EDITOR: LEE J

MW00608888

ELITE S ~~ELITE S~~

UN FORCES
1948-94

Text by
ROBERT PITTA
Colour plates by
SIMON McCOUAIG

First published in Great Britain in 1994
by Osprey, an imprint of Reed Consumer Books Limited
Michelin House, 81 Fulham Road,
London SW3 6RB
and Auckland, Melbourne, Singapore and Toronto

© Copyright 1994 Reed International Books Limited

All rights reserved. Apart from any fair dealing for the
purpose of private study, research, criticism or review, as
permitted under the Copyright Designs and Patents Act,
1988, no part of this publication may be reproduced,
stored in a retrieval system, or transmitted in any form or
by any means, electronic, electrical, chemical,
mechanical, optical, photocopying, recording or
otherwise, without the prior permission of the copyright
owner. Enquiries should be addressed to the Publishers.

ISBN 1 85532 4547

Filmset in Great Britain by Keyspools Ltd, Lancashire
Printed through Bookbuilders Ltd, Hong Kong

Artist's note

Readers may care to note that the original paintings from
which the colour plates in this book were prepared are
available for private sale. All reproduction copyright
whatsoever is retained by the publisher. All enquiries
should be addressed to:

Simon McCouaig
4 Yeoman's Close
Stoke Bishop
Bristol BS9 1DH

The publishers regret that they can enter into no
correspondence upon this matter.

For a catalogue of all books published by Osprey Military
please write to:

The Marketing Manager,
Consumer Catalogue Department,
Osprey Publishing Ltd,
Michelin House, 81 Fulham Road,
London SW3 6RB

Acknowledgements and Author's Note

The author would like to thank the following individuals and
organizations for their assistance: US National Archives; Bob
Waller, DoD Still Media Records Center; United Nations
Information Office, Washington, DC; Ms. Joyce Rosenblum,
United Nations, New York; Lt.Col. Juhani Loikaanen, Per-
manent Mission of Finland to the United Nations; Ms. Sonya
Lundquist, Swedish Armed Forces International Centre;
Paratus Magazine; Jeff Fannell; Richard McAroy; Chuck
Melson; George Peterson; and W.E. Storey.

   The end of the Cold War and the demise of
superpower confrontation have brought an era of co-
operation and the hope of a 'New World Order' that has
thrust the United Nations, whether ready or not, into the
forefront of world conflict resolution. The number of on-
going operations is steadily growing, as are the cost and the
violence involved. The UN role is also in transition, moving
from peace-keeping to peace-making, with humanitarian
efforts seen on a large scale. This book is limited, however,
to a discussion of the background, establishment, and
activities of the more visible, largest, and most recent peace-
keeping force and military observer missions. Special
emphasis is placed on recent missions. The UN role in the
Korean and Gulf Wars, the distinctive uniforms of the UN
participants, and specific insignia developed for these forces
are also described.

Publisher's note

Readers may wish to study this title in conjunction with the
following Osprey publications:

MAA 127 *The Israeli Army in the Middle East Wars
   1948–73*
MAA 128 *Arab Armies of the Middle East Wars 1948–
   73*
MAA 142 *Partisan Warfare 1941–45*
MAA 165 *Armies in Lebanon 1982–1984*
MAA 174 *The Korean War 1950–53*
MAA 194 *Arab Armies of the Middle East Wars (2)*
MAA 209 *The War in Cambodia 1970–75*
MAA 221 *Central American Wars 1959–89*
MAA 242 *Modern African Wars 3*
Desert Storm Special 1 *Land Power – The Coalition
   and Iraqi Armies*
Desert Storm Special 2 *Air Power – The Coalition and
   Iraqi Air Forces*
Desert Storm Special 3 – *Sea Power – The Coalition
   and Iraqi Navies*

INTRODUCTION

The Charter of the United Nations Organization (UNO) lists the UN's main purpose as the maintenance of international peace and security, the taking of effective collective measures for the prevention and removal of threats to peace, the suppression of acts of aggression, and the peaceful settlement of international disputes or situations that might lead to a breach of peace. The principal bodies of the UN involved in peace-making and peace-keeping are the General Assembly and the Security Council.

The General Assembly, made up of representatives of 162 nation states each entrusted with one vote, is the world's forum for discussing matters that affect world peace and security and for making recommendations concerning them. On questions regarding international peace and security a two-thirds majority of members must be present and voting. The Assembly can make recommendations to member nations and to the Security Council. The Assembly also participates in international programmes concerning economic, social, cultural, educational, health, and human rights issues.

The Security Council is the main body vested with responsibility for the establishment and maintenance of international peace and security. Its functions are outlined in Chapters 6 and 7 of the UN Charter as: to prevent war by settling disputes between nations, to recommend appropriate methods or procedures to reach a settlement, and to recommend actual terms of a settlement. The Council has five permanent members (United States, Soviet Union/Russia, Great Britain, France, and China), and ten temporary members each elected by the Assembly for two-year terms. A nine-vote majority is needed to carry a proposal. Under the UN Charter the Council is permitted to call for economic sanctions (under Article 41) or, in extreme cases, to dispatch a military force to stop aggression (under Article 42).

All member nations have armed forces, facilities, and other forms of assistance ready and available to the Council to maintain peace. UN peace-keeping operations are divided into two broad categories: observer missions, consisting of unarmed military officers; and peace-

Major Crute (centre) of the Australian contingent to UNTSO confers with Jordan Police Corporal Khalil (left) and UNTSO Security Officer Anderson (right) at the Tulkarm outstation on the Jordanian side of the Jordan-Israeli border, May 1959. Of interest is Major Crute's use of the blue beret with both UN metal insignia and Royal Australian Artillery insignia. (United Nations)

keeping forces, consisting of lightly armed infantry and armoured units with support elements. For specific purposes observer missions can be reinforced by infantry/support units, while peace-keeping forces can be assisted by unarmed military observers. Analysis of peace-keeping operations reveals that certain factors are fundamental to the success, or failure, of such UN involvement. Firstly, it is necessary for all factions, and all countries involved in the UN effort, to agree to the establishment of the peace-keeping operation. Secondly, the peace-keeping operation must not interfere with either the impartiality of the UN forces, or the internal affairs of the host country. Finally, the conflicting factions must co-operate with the UN forces and allow them freedom of movement. The UN rules of engagement state that force should only be used in self-defence or as a last resort (the first peace-keeping mission mandated under Chapter 7 of the UN charter, allowing the use of offensive force to achieve the objectives of UN resolutions, was put into effect in Somali/UNOSOM in 1992).

EARLY OPERATIONS

The first peace-keeping operation in the Middle East was conducted by the United Nations Truce Supervision Organization (UNTSO) formed during the 1948 Arab–Israeli War. UNTSO's first task was to supervise the Palestine truce. At that time Palestine administered by the United Kingdom under a League of Nations mandate, had a population of 1.5 million Arabs and 500,000 Jews. The United Nations General Assembly proposed a plan, which was quickly rejected, to partition the territory into separate Arab and Jewish states, with the city of Jerusalem placed under international control. On 14 May 1948 the United Kingdom relinquished its mandate over Palestine, and the state of Israel was

proclaimed. On 15 May the Palestinian Arabs, assiste by the armies of other Arab states, attacked the newl formed republic.

The UN Security Council, in Resolution 50 (2 May 1948), called for a cessation of hostilities i Palestine. The truce was to be supervised by the UI Truce Supervision Organisation (UNTSO), this cor sisted of a UN mediator and military observers. At th time UNTSO had an authorized strength of 572. Wit the agreement of both parties the first UNTSO observe arrived in the area on 11 June 1948.

The UNTSO observers were initially used t supervise the original truce of 1948, but after numerot General Armistice Agreements were signed betwee Israel and Egypt, Jordan, Lebanon, and Syria th supervision of these new agreements became paramoun Around this time UNTSO Headquarters were estal lished at Government House in Jerusalem. Following th 1967 war UNTSO was involved in cease-fire observatio in the Israeli-Syria sector and along the Suez Cana Similar operations were established in southern Leban in 1973, in the Sinai in 1973, the Golan Heights in 197 and in southern Lebanon in 1978.

The UNTSO Observer Group Golan (OGG) detacl ment is assigned to the United Nations Disengageme Observer Force (UNDOF) on the Golan Heights in th Israeli-Syria sector. The OGG occupy eleven observatio posts and conduct area inspections every two weeks. Th Observer Detachment Damascus (ODD), also assigned UNTSO, performs support functions for the OGG Syria. In the Israel-Lebanon sector the UNTSO Observ Group Lebanon (OGL) operates along with the Unit Nations Interim Force in Lebanon (UNIFIL), maintai ing five observation posts on the Lebanese side of th agreed demarcation line. The OGL also maintains fi mobile observer teams in the area under Israeli contro The UNTSO Observer Group Egypt (OGE) maintai forces in the Egypt-Israeli sector, headquartered Ismailia, with outposts in the Sinai.

UNTSO personnel have contributed to the orga

United Nations shoulder sleeve insignia, from left to right: silver bullion embroidered on light blu wool (7cm diameter); white thread hand-embroidered on light blu wool (7cm diameter); anc machine-embroidered white thread on medium blue wool (8cm diameter (Author's photo)

Korea 1950–53

The UN Security Council met on 25 June 1950 to consider the invasion of South Korea by the North, and passed a resolution calling upon the North to cease hostilities and withdraw. A second resolution was passed on 27 June requesting member assistance to South Korea. The Soviet Union had boycotted the Council since January in protest at Nationalist China's occupation of a seat on the Council despite their eviction from the Chinese mainland by the communists, and thus missed an opportunity to veto the resolutions made against their client state North Korea. The Soviets subsequently claimed that the Korean conflict was an internal one, and that UN decisions were illegal since neither the Soviet Union nor Communist China were present at the Council meeting. The US held that the UN was morally committed to helping South Korea, though not a member state, since the UN had created the state by supervising the 1948 Korean elections. While the UN debate raged President Truman committed troops to the area to cover the evacuation of US citizens on 26 June. As the situation deteriorated, General Douglas MacArthur was authorized to commit US ground forces on 30 June, while Australia, New Zealand, and the United Kingdom placed naval forces at the disposal of UN command. A resolution passed on 7 July recommended placing all UN forces under a unified command with the US requested to nominate a commander. The UN Command was formally established on 14 July under the command of General MacArthur, with 42 out of 59 member states providing some sort of assistance. Fifteen countries provided troops, and five countries medical units.

All UN forces, except for British Commonwealth ground troops, were put under US command. A major UN requirement was to rebuild the South Korean (ROK) forces, which lacked equipment and training. Not until 1951, when the front lines stabilized, could efforts

t.Col. Bore (seated) of 'rance and Capt. wartling of Sweden, both iembers of UNTSO, bserving activity along 'he west side of the Suez

Canal from position 'Op Yellow' on the eastern bank in Israeli-occupied Sinai, April 1973. (United Nations/Y. Nagata)

ation and establishment of UN peace-keeping and bserver missions unconnected to the Arab-Israeli roblem. In 1960 experienced UNTSO military observ- 's assisted in the UN Operation in the Congo (ONUC), 1963 with the UN Yemen Observation Mission JNYOM), in 1988 with the UN Good Offices Mission Afghanistan and Pakistan (UNGOMAP) and the UN an-Iraq Military Observer Group (UNIIMOG), in 991 with the UN Iraq-Kuwait Observation Mission JNIKOM), and in 1992 with the UN Protection Force JNPROFOR) and the UN Operation in Mozambique JNUMOZ).

/M Sherry of the South frican Air Force painting e distinctive flying heetah emblem of 2 quadron SAAF on an F- 'D Mustang, while US

Army Corporal Schneider, sporting the emblem on his field jacket, watches; Korea, 1951. (Paratus Magazine)

Above: US Marines on a reconnaissance mission return to their rendezvous point for pick up by a Navy Martin PB-5 Mariner, 1950. (US Marine Corps)

Canadian troops arrive in Yokohama, Japan, en route to the fighting in Korea, July 1951. (US Army)

Belgian and British officers ride an armoured vehicle to reach the front lines at Hill 88 north of the Imjin River, Korea, June 1951. (US Army)

made to re-equip the ROK forces, which totalled [...]0,000 men by the end of the war.

The contributions of UN members, other than the [U]S, totalled 40,000 ground personnel, 1,100 airmen, [...]68 medical staff, and 30,000 naval personnel. By the [en]d of the war the US had committed 302,483 ground [tr]oops (the total forces under UN command totalled [...]2,539, including ROK forces). US casualties totalled [...]2,091 (33,000 deaths); the South Koreans suffered [...]0,000, and other UN members 17,260 casualties.

An armistice was signed on 27 July 1953, thereby [ful]filling the Security Council resolutions calling upon [me]mber assistance to South Korea to force the North to [cea]se hostilities and withdraw from the South. The UN [Co]mmand in Korea still exists, consisting of a token [for]ce from each nation that committed troops to the [figh]ting, to carry out the armistice terms. Some of these [nat]ions maintained troop commitments in South Korea [for] decades, with the Royal Thai Army the last to leave [in] June 1972 (the US still maintains a large presence in [the] country). Periodically North Korean allies attempt to [dis]solve the UN Command, which meets regularly at [Pa]nmunjom to discuss numerous cease-fire violations. [Th]ough there has never been a formal peace treaty the [U]N resolutions were fulfilled. The Korean War cannot [be] considered a UN peace-keeping operation since the [acti]ons were not carried out by the UN itself, the [con]sent of both belligerents to UN involvement was not [gra]nted, and force was used to fulfil the UN mandate.

First United Nations Emergency Force (UNEF I)

In 1955, despite the efforts of the UNTSO Chief of Staff and the Secretary General, relations between Egypt and Israel deteriorated. This was the result of frequent raids by Palestinian *fedayeen* who were supported by Egypt, into Israel, and the increasingly violent reprisal attacks by the Israeli Defense Forces. At this time both Egypt and Israel were engaged in a massive arms build-up brought on by the heightening of tensions caused by Egypt's restriction of Israeli traffic through the Suez Canal.

In July 1956 the United States withdrew support for the Aswan Dam project on the Nile, prompting President Nasser to announce the nationalization of the Suez Canal Company with the intention of using Canal dues to finance the dam project. The Security Council was asked to consider the issue, and adopted a resolution allowing free and open transit through the Canal. Before further discussion could commence Israel attacked Egypt in October 1956. France and the United Kingdom, in a joint ultimatum to both parties, requested a cessation of hostilities and the stationing of Anglo-French forces along the Canal to separate the belligerents and ensure the safety of shipping. When Egypt rejected the ultimatum Anglo-French forces launched air assaults against Egyptian targets and landed troops at the northern end of the Canal. Numerous resolutions, proposed by both the United States and the Soviet Union, to end the fighting were submitted to the Security Council and voted down by France and the United Kingdom. An emergency session of the General Assembly proposed by the United States called for an immediate cease-fire, the re-opening of the Canal, the withdrawal of all forces, and the creation of a United Nations Emergency Force (UNEF, later to be known as UNEF I) to secure and supervise the armistice with an authorized strength of 6,073.

The cease-fire was established on 7 November 1956, and UNEF took up positions in a buffer zone between the Anglo-French and the Egyptian forces, and in Port Said; when the Anglo-French forces withdrew on 22 December UNEF took over their positions. UNEF maintained the cease-fire and arranged Israel's withdrawal, carried out prisoner exchanges, repaired damaged roads, and cleared mines from the Sinai. On 16 May 1967 the Egyptian government requested the withdrawal of UNEF from Egypt's borders and the Gaza Strip. Israel rejected a UN request for UNEF maintenance of the Buffer Zone from Israeli territory. UNEF was then withdrawn from the area. The ten-year mission was successful, but cost the lives of 90 peace-keepers.

Second United Nations Emergency Force (UNEF II)

In a surprise co-ordinated move, on 6 October 1973 Egyptian forces crossed the Suez Canal and advanced through the observation points of UNTSO, while Syrian troops simultaneously attacked Israeli positions on the Golan Heights. By 9 October all UN observation posts in the area were closed and UN forces withdrawn. On 23 October the Security Council called for a cease-fire. A request by Egypt for a joint US-Soviet peace-keeping force was not granted due to US-Soviet differences. To stabilize this volatile situation, on 27 October the Security Council approved plans for the establishment of a new United Nations Emergency Force (later known as UNEF II), with an authorized strength of approximately 7,000. On 27 October, with the assistance of UNTSO observers, UNEF established posts and checkpoints in the area, thereby stabilizing the situation and observing the cease-fire agreed at a UN-sponsored meeting held at kilometre marker 109 on the Cairo-Suez road.

During this time Dr. Henry Kissinger, the United States representative, engaged in 'shuttle diplomacy' between the two countries. Kissinger attempted to work out agreements as to troop positioning, prisoners of war, and the UN separation and observation of each side. Additional mediation efforts took place, including a peace conference in Geneva. It was not until 18 January 1974, at a meeting held at kilometre 101 on the Cairo-Suez road and presided over by Dr. Kissinger, that agreement was reached for the deployment of Egyptian and Israeli forces, the establishment of a UNEF-controlled buffer zone and demilitarized zones along the Canal. This agreement was put into effect on 25 January and completed without major incident on 5 March. Further negotiations in September 1975 resulted in the redeployment of forces, the re-establishment of buffer zones, a UN-sponsored joint commission to resolve problems that might arise, and a United States established and manned early warning system in the Gida and Mitla Passes. A final peace treaty was signed in March 1979 between Egypt and Israel under the Camp

The first group of Finnish peace-keepers to deploy to the Sinai as part of UNEF in 1956. (Finnish Ministry of Defence)

Finnish Battalion member of UNEF manning a position at a former Egyptian missile site destroyed by withdrawing Israeli forces in the southern boundary of the second-phase buffer zone, February 1974. (United Nations/Y. Nagata)

Below: A typical UNTSO observation post, OP FOXTROT, located on the West side of the Suez Canal. Observing movement on the East side are Commander E. Nunes of Chile (left) and Major A. Proud of Argentina (right), April 1973. (United Nations/Y Nagata)

David Accords. Strong opposition to the Accords from the PLO, Arab states, and the Soviet Union, coupled with the Israeli withdrawal from the northern Sinai under the peace treaty, prompted the Security Council to allow the mandate of UNEF to lapse on 24 July 1979. UNEF personnel withdrew from the northern part of the buffer zone and Egyptian forces took control in the area.

THE CONGO

The Congo (now Zaire), the third largest country in Africa with almost a million square miles of territory, holds vast mineral deposits. King Leopold II of Belgium obtained title to the territory in 1885 and took over administration of the colony. The sweeping changes affecting other African colonies after the Second World War had little effect on the Congo. The Belgian colonial administration was lax in providing political and educational advancement. In 1959, in reponse to numerous disturbances, the Belgian government announced a plan for the independence of their colony; municipal council elections held in December, with full independence promised by 30 June 1960. A treaty of friendship between Belgium and the Congo was signed, allowing administrative and technical personnel of the colonial regime to stay on to ensure a smooth transition to

Radio Operator Sgt. Ali, of the Tunisian contingent to the UN Force in the Congo (ONUC), monitors radio communications in Luluabourg, September 1960. (United Nations)

the government led by President Joseph Kasavubu and Premier Patrice Lumumba. Two military bases were ceded to the Belgians so that their troops could, at the request of the Congolese government, assist in the maintenance of law and order. A 25,000-man Congolese security force, the Force Publique, led by Belgian officers under Lt.Gen. Emile Janssens, was expected to maintain order as it had done during colonial times. UN Secretary-General Dag Hammarskjöld, after a January 1960 visit to the area, saw the need for additional assistance and, through Under Secretary Ralph Bunch, the details were worked out for a UN assistance programme.

Shortly after independence the Force Publique Congolese troops petitioned for higher pay and benefits. On 5 July 1960 this petition was denied by Gen. Janssens, causing the Leopoldville (now Kinshasa) garrison to mutiny. Fighting quickly spread to other areas; looting and increasingly violent attacks against Belgians and other Europeans caused large numbers of Belgian administrators to flee the country, and essential services collapsed country-wide. President Lumumba refused to request the assistance of the locally stationed Belgian troops, and agreed to meet the demands of the

Force Publique. He renamed the Force the Armé Nationale Congolese (ANC), dismissed Gen. Janssen and attempted to nationalize the force with the appoin ment of both a Congolese commander, Maj.Gen. Vict Lundula, and a Chief of Staff, Col. Joseph Mobut while giving all ranks a one grade promotion. In spite these concessions, disorder spread and increased. On July, due to the negotiations of Ralph Bunch, t Congolese government agreed to a plan where U military personnel, acting as technical advisers, would deployed to the country to help control and strengthe the Congolese Army. It was hoped that this would enab the army to maintain law and order. On 11 July, withou the agreement of the Congolese government, Belgiu ordered its troops into the country to restore law an order and protect Belgian nationals. Belgian troop landed at Leopoldville, Lulabourg (now Kananga Elisabethville (now Lubumbashi), and Matadi, wher heavy fighting with Congolese troops increased t widespread chaos. On the same day Moise Tshomb Premier of the mineral-rich Katanga Province (whic provided the country with over half its revenues seceded from the republic; the province of South Kas soon followed Tshombe's lead.

On 12 July the Congolese government officially r quested UN military assistance to protect the territory the Congo against the external threat represented Belgian intervention. On 14 July the Security Counc adopted Resolution 143 (1960) which called for the estal lishment of the United Nations Operation in the Cong (ONUC); the withdrawal of Belgian troops; and milita assistance to the government of the Republic of the Cong The UN force was to be regarded as temporary an impartial, deployed with the consent of the governme until local forces could restore order. It aimed to establis freedom of movement throughout the country; using forc only in self-defence; and was to be built around a core contingents from African nations. The first contingen comprised seven battalions totalling 4,000 men fro Ethiopia, Ghana, Guinea, Morocco, and Tunisia. T Swedish battalion of the United Nations Emergency For (UNEF) in Gaza was temporarily transferred to ONU with light aircraft, communications, and logistic suppo provided by non–African nations.

Attempted restoration of law and order

The Belgian government stated that they had no desig on the Congo and would withdraw from the area whe ONUC had restored law and order. When the first U troops were deployed in Leopoldville, at the power an radio stations and along the major roads, on the evenin of 15 July a sense of calm returned to the city.

ponse to the UN deployment, Belgian troops were hdrawn to their barracks. Though the ONUC ployment was carried out quickly, the Congolese ernment issued an ultimatum on 17 July stating that he Belgian forces were not completely withdrawn in hours they would request troops from the Soviet ion. The deployment continued with all Belgian ops withdrawn from Leopoldville by 23 July and from entire Congo, except Katanga, by August without itional posturing by the Congolese government.

The problem in Katanga worsened, and President mumba requested ONUC assistance in quelling the ellion; the UN mandate did not allow for this istance and the request was refused. The Katangese osed ONUC entry into their territory while the gians, citing this opposition, would not withdraw ir forces from the area. Secretary-General Ham- rskjöld made a second trip to Leopoldville on 4 gust 1960 in preparation for the entry of UN troops Katanga. This entry was postponed due to the lent opposition of the Katangese, forcing the Secre- General to seek a Security Council resolution. olution 146 (1960) was passed on 9 August, calling the immediate withdrawal of Belgian troops and the ry of ONUC troops into Katanga (without interven- in the internal conflict). On 12 August the Secretary neral returned to the Congo and personally led the UC forces into Katanga, the Belgian forces peacefully ndrawing in response.

In August the internal situation worsened; long- ding rivalries between Baluba and Lulua tribesmen ed up, and the Baluba declared the secession of South ai Province. In Equator and Leopoldville Provinces

opposition to the government gained strength. The Congolese government arrested opposition leaders, closed down newspapers, and sent ANC troops into the area who subsequently killed many civilians, including women and children. These ANC actions led ONUC to try to protect the threatened people of the region but without using force, as mandated, even when UN personnel were attacked. The atrocities which accompanied much of the chaotic fighting in the Congo continued to cause widespread concern in the Western world, adding to the pressure on the UN to solve problems for which it was not organized or equipped.

Constitutional Crisis

On 5 September 1960 President Kasavubu dismissed Prime Minister Lumumba; Lumumba refused to leave his post and dismissed Kasavubu as Chief of State. The parliament supported Lumumba, though would not endorse the dismissal of Kasavubu. Kasavubu then dismissed parliament. Col. Mobutu instigated a coup to install an army-backed regime in support of Kasavubu on 14 September. In response ONUC closed down Leopoldville airport to prevent the arrival of additional Congolese faction troops; temporarily closed the radio station to quell broadcasts inciting numerous violent riots; and honoured requests by all factions for ONUC protection of faction leaders. In South Kasai ONUC arranged a cease fire between the ANC and secessionists, established a neutral zone under UN control, and convinced the ANC to withdraw from the Katanga border. In Katanga ONUC established neutral zones to separate the warring factions, and protected and evacuated numerous Europeans who were threatened by the

wedish member of UC on duty at a UN- intained refugee camp dies Swahili with camp dren, Elisabethville, go; September 1961. As sult of the fighting in anga Province over 00 Congolese were de refugees and sought assistance. (United ions)

ONUC troops at a bridge over the Lufira River constructing a provision bridge using empty oil drums to enable troops continue operations; Katanga, January 1963. (United Nations)

violence. On 8 November an ONUC Irish contingent was ambushed in northern Katanga, leaving eight dead. On 24 November ANC troops attacked the Ghanaian embassy, injuring many and killing one ONUC Tunisian contingent member. Despite ONUC's efforts the country was turned into an armed camp with four opposing factions.

On the night of 27/28 November Lumumba attempted to flee his ONUC-guarded residence to Stanleyville, his stronghold; arrested by Mobutu-backed ANC troops near Port Fracqui, he was transferred to Elisabethville in Katanga on 17 January 1961, and subsequently killed. Lumumba's death triggered a series of reprisals and counter-reprisals, causing the civil war to widen. The Security Council met on 15 February 1961 and adopted Resolution 16 authorizing the use of force, as a last resort, to prevent the civil war from spreading; the evacuation of all foreign nationals not under UN command; and the withdrawal of mercenary forces. ONUC was deployed throughout the country, but was unable to fulfil its mandate due to the withdrawal of 5,000 ONUC troops by their governments and the increasing hostility of the Congolese factions.

In April 1961 the civil war in northern Katanga province flared up, when the Katangese gendarmerie, led by foreign mercenaries, launched an offensive to destroy the anti-Tshombe forces. After a UN warning on 27 March to cease hostilities was ignored, ONUC intervened militarily, checked Katangese operations and established control in the area. Further ONUC casualties were incurred, including the ambush and massacre of 44 Ghanaian members at Port Fracqui in late April, and the killing of 13 Italian aircrew at Kindu on 11 November.

After numerous failed conferences on 22 July 1961

Kasavubu reconvened parliament, with ONUC assistance and protection; 200 out of 221 members attended. A government of national unity was constituted on August under Prime Minister Cyrille Adoula.

Termination of Katangese Secession

ONUC's efforts to eliminate foreign interference Katanga province were largely successful. Nevertheless the withdrawl of the Belgians, enabled Tshombe's regime to consolidate power in southern Katanga, but not without the assistance of foreign mercenaries, powerful fore financial and political interests, and large quantities weapons purchased from foreign governments. Tshombe launched an ethnic cleansing campaign against his political and tribal enemies. In April 1961, after ONUC's reinforcement, Tshombe's representatives accepted Resolution 161 (21 February 1961), and large numbers of foreign soldiers of fortune were repatriated out of the country beginning in June 1961. A group of mercenaries infiltrated into Katanga, organized and armed gendarmerie forces, and persuaded Tshombe to attack ONUC. On 13 September these forces attacked the Belgian consulate in Elisabethville, the UN base at Kamina and the UN garrison in Albertville. The fighting grew more intense, and a mercenary-piloted jet fighter wreaked havoc on ONUC ground forces and disabled ONUC light transport aircraft; the UN did not deploy offensive weapons such as fighter aircraft or tanks since they were incompatible with the UN mandate. During this period Secretary-General Hammarskjöld travelled to Leopoldville to bring about a reconciliation between the warring parties, and flew to Northern Rhodesia to meet Tshombe on 17 September; the UN aircraft crashed en route killing the Secretary General, the Swedish flight crew, and several

ONUC Swedish [ar]moured personnel [car]rier crosses the [Lu]kama Railroad Bridge, [stil]l under repair by the [Sw]edish 20th Battalion [and] Congolese National [Rail]way; Bukama, Congo, [Sep]tember 1963. After two [yea]rs of interruption the [rai]l line was re-opened [bet]ween the Province of [Ka]tanga and the rest of [the] country. (United [Na]tions)

[U]N staff members. Other UN representatives took up [Ha]mmarskjöld's mission and a military ceasefire was [sign]ed on 20 September.

At first, in accordance with the agreement, numer-[ous] prisoners were exchanged and troops withdrawn to [previ]ous positions. However Tshombe's regime soon [bro]ke with the agreement, demanding independence, and [lau]nching mercenary-led land and air raids which [ON]UC was unable to counter. Resolution 169 (24 [No]vember 1961) authorized the use of force to remove [an] estimated 237 mercenaries from Katanga. In response [Tsh]ombe launched a propaganda campaign against the [UN] resulting in the abduction and murder of numerous [UN] personnel. On 5 December 1961 the Katangese [gen]darmerie established road blocks hindering ONUC [free]dom of movement, and attempted to isolate and [dest]roy the UN forces in Elisabethville. By 15 December [ON]UC had received reinforcements, seizing control of [the] road blocks and other positions within three days. By [18] December, having consolidated its positions, ONUC [dec]lared a truce and relative calm returned to the area. [Th]e UN forces then assisted the local police in their [effo]rt to stop looting and restore law and order.

A meeting in Kitona between Tshombe and Prime [Min]ister Adoula on 20 December culminated in the sign-[ing] of an eight-point declaration, under this Tshombe [agre]ed to recognize the central government in [Leo]poldville, to end the secession of Katanga, and to [resp]ect UN resolutions. This declaration was only ac-[cep]ted by the Katanga Assembly as a basis for discussions [with] the central government; further attempts at a resolu-[tion] through discussion failed and the talks were sus-[pen]ded in June 1962. In response to the breakdown of talks [Secr]etary-General U Thant proposed, with member na-

tion approval, a plan for reconciliation in the Congo which was eventually accepted by both Tshombe and Adoula. This provided for a federalist-type government, a division of revenues between the central and provincial govern-ments, unification of all military and paramilitary forces into a national army, a central currency, a general amnesty, a reconstruction of the central government, and freedom of movement for UN forces country-wide. After accep-tance of the plan the Katangese made no effort to imple-ment it and, before economic sanctions could be imposed on the province, attacked ONUC forces on 11 December.

The ONUC forces did not return fire for six days, but, when negotiation had no effect, they launched counter-operations against the Katangese. By 30 Dec-ember 1962 ONUC Ethiopian, Indian, and Irish troops had gained control of a 20-mile radius around Elisabethville while Ghanaian and Swedish troops occupied Kamina. On 31 December ONUC Indian troops moved toward Jadotville (now Likasi), crossing the Lufira River to reach their destination by 3 January 1963. By 4 January ONUC troops had established their presence in Elisabethville, Kamina, Jadotville, and Kipushi, where basic services were restored to the local populations. Tshombe fled to Kolwezi, where he announced on 14 January his intent to end the secession movement and to accept implementation of the national reconciliation plan, requesting amnesty as provided for under the plan. On 21 January, after agreement by all parties, ONUC entered Katanga. The Katangese attempt at secession was ended.

Consolidation of the Congolese Government

The end of Katangese secession brought added responsi-bilities for the UN civilian programmes that had been in operation since 1960. Essential public services were restored; loans guaranteed to the government; refugee relief efforts expanded; training in agriculture, labour, and public services restored; and a rebuilding of the infrastructure re-initiated. On 4 February 1963 the Secretary General reported that the territorial integrity and political independence of the Congo had been maintained, law and order restored, and a reduction in ONUC personnel was proceeding. On 27 July 1963 Resolution 1876 established the last day of 1963 as the termination date for the ONUC military forces. A Congolese government request for the force to remain until 20 June 1964 was agreed (Resolution 1885) on 18 October 1963. The United Nations Operation in the Congo withdrew from the country on 20 June. A small programme of UN technical assistance continued under the Office of the Resident Representative of the United Nations Development Program.

ONUC was, at the time, the largest mission established by the UN, comprising a military force and civilian component of 20,000 personnel. Originally mandated to provide military and administrative services following the Belgian intervention, ONUC became involved in a confused and violent civil war. The UN involvement conflicted with the priorities of the Soviet Union and other powers, led to the death of Secretary-General Dag Hammarskjöld, created a political and financial crisis for the UN, and cost the lives of 234 ONUC personnel.

POST CONGO OPERATIONS

The Republic of Cyprus became independent on August 1960 with a constitution based on agreeme reached on 11 February 1959 by Greece, Turkey, United Kingdom, and agreed upon by the island's Gr and Turkish Cypriot communities. The 1959 settlem recognized the ethnic composition of the island (8 Greek and 18% Turkish); sought to maintain a bala between the two communities' rights and interests, w Greece, Turkey, and the United Kingdom as guaran of the articles of the constitution; established the righ each guarantor to take action to maintain the settlem forbade the union of Cyprus with any other state, or partitioning of the island; and permitted United Ki dom sovereignty of two areas to be maintained military bases. The application of the constituti provisions proved difficult and led to rising tens between the leaders of the two Cypriot communities.

Following the rejection of a number of proposal modify the constitution made by the Greek Cyp leader, President Archbishop Makarios, mutual acc ations abounded, leading to violence on the island or December 1963. On 24 December the Turkish mili contingent stationed in Cyprus under the terms of agreement left camp, and established a presence northern Nicosia, where disturbances had erup Reports of Turkish military over-flights of the military concentrations along the Turkish southern co and naval movements added to the tension on the isla On 27 December the Security Council met to consid complaint by Cyprus charging aggression and interv tion in Cypriot internal affairs by Turkey. Tur maintained that Greek Cypriot leaders were attemp to nullify Turkish Cypriot rights and denied aggression. The situation degenerated rapidly, w scattered intercommunal fighting, heavy casualties, h tage-taking and kidnappings, irregular force ambus the break-down of government, and the rising threa military intervention by either Greece or Turkey.

After all attempts to restore peace had failed, Security Council adopted Resolution 186 on 4 M 1964, recommending the establishment of the Un

Since 1964 the Greek and Turkish Cypriot communities have been separated by a 180-kilometre-long buffer zone controlled by

UNFICYP. Here Danis contingent members patrol the buffer zone i Ferret armoured car, November 1990. (Unite Nations/J. Isaac)

ations Peace-keeping Force in Cyprus (UNFICYP) with a mandate to prevent the recurrence of fighting, to maintain law and order, and to promote a return to normal conditions. UNFICYP had an authorized strength of 6411, and was established for a period of three months with a review and re-authorization by the Security Council at the end of that period. The UN contingents were deployed throughout the island in areas of responsibility that matched the island's established administrative boundaries, ensuring close working relationships between the UN and Cypriot government officials. In Nicosia UN troops took up observation posts along a so-called 'green line', while other UN troops established patrol and observation routines in areas of tension. Despite the deployment of UN troops sporadic violence continued, with occasional periods of heavy fighting.

In March 1970 the underlying tension within the Greek community increased with an attempt on the life of President Makarios and the killing of the former Minister of the Interior. Clandestine activity by factions supporting the union of Cyprus with Greece continued into 1971. On 15 July 1974 the Cypriot National Guard, under the direct orders of mainland Greek officers, staged a coup d'état against the government of President Makarios. On 20 July the Turkish government, citing the 1960 treaty, launched a major military operation against northern Cyprus, occupying the main Turkish Cypriot enclave and surrounding areas. Despite UNFICYP attempts to promote a cease-fire, intensive fighting broke out in the vicinity of Nicosia International Airport. The National Guard reacted to the Turkish landings with attacks on Turkish Cypriot areas throughout the island. UNFICYP attempted to arrange local cease-fire agreements, and was heavily involved in the 21 July evacuation of foreign nationals, while maintaining observation over the battle zones.

On 30 July, in response to Security Council Resolution 353 (1974), the representatives of Greece, Turkey, and the United Kingdom agreed upon a 16 August *de facto* cease-fire that included UN inspection of the warring forces, an establishment of cease-fire lines, establishment of a buffer zone between the warring nations, and adherence to the military status quo in the buffer zone. The buffer zone eventually extended 180 miles across the island, varying in width from 20 metres to seven kilometres, and it is under constant UNIFCYP surveillance from 150 observation posts and air, vehicular and foot patrols. Each year hundreds of incidents are reported, the most serious in areas where the cease-fire lines are close, as in Nicosia.

Growing international impatience with the lack of

An Austrian member of UNDOF patrolling on Mt.Hermon, December 1975. (United Nations/Y. Nagata)

progress in re-uniting the Greek and Turkish Cypriot factions was a major factor in the June 1993 decision by the Canadian Government to withdraw their forces, less than one year after the Danish contingent left the island, thus ending 29 years of Canadian participation in UNFICYP. These withdrawals reduced the UNFICYP force by over one-third.

United Nations Disengagement Observer Force (UNDOF)

On 6 October 1973 war broke out between the Egyptian and Israeli forces in the Suez Canal area and the Sinai Peninsula, and between Israeli and Syrian forces on the Golan Heights. At the height of the fighting in mid-October the Security Council established a second United Nations Emergency Force (UNEF II) which was moved into the Suez Canal area, separating the Israeli and Egyptian forces. In March 1974 the situation became destabilized to the point that the United States undertook a bold diplomatic initiative; this resulted in a formal agreement of disengagement between the Israeli and Syrian forces, providing two equal zones of separation each containing limited military forces and armaments. UN Security Council Resolution 350 established the United Nations Disengagement Observer Force (UNDOF) in the Golan Heights to monitor the situation and maintain the cease-fire between Israel and Syria, to supervise the disengagement of these forces, and to supervise the areas of separation. UNDOF's mandate has been extended for periods of six months at a time.

On 3 June 1974 UN advance parties arrived in the area and the total authorized strength of 1,250 was soon reached. After completion of the initial disengagement operation and the establishment of areas of separation a series of UNDOF checkpoints and observations posts were created, with two base camps, one on each side of the separation line. In each area of separation UNDOF maintains static observation posts and positions, manned 24 hours a day, where vehicle or foot patrols operate. Syria maintains police patrols in its area to monitor the growing influx of civilians. With the assistance of liason officers from both sides UNDOF conducts bi-monthly inspections of armaments and military force levels in each area. Full reports of the findings are made available to all parties.

UNDOF routinely provides humanitarian support, including the transfer of released prisoners of war and the remains of war dead, the exchange of mail, the passage of civilians across the area of separation, and medical treatment to the civilian population.

Since 1977 there have been no major incidents involving UNDOF; the situation in the Israeli-Syria sector has remained relatively quiet, and UNDOF has continued to accomplish its mission with the co-operation of all parties.

United Nations Interim Force in Lebanon (UNIFIL)

At the end of the Lebanese Civil War in October 1975 in spite of the election of President Sarkis, the establis ment of a constitution and central government, and t creation of an Arab Deterrent Force (ADF) to ensure t peace – fighting still raged in southern Lebano Tensions increased when the Syrian contingent to t ADF deployed southward, leading the Israeli Gover ment to threaten countermeasures if the ADF proceed beyond a 'red line' south of the Zahrani River. Thou the Syrian forces stopped short of the 'red line', fighti between Christian militias aligned with Israel and a lo coalition of Muslim and Leftist parties, collectiv named the Lebanese National Movement and aided the Palestine Liberation Organization (PLO), continu unabated in the south. The PLO launched repea commando raids against Israel, culminating in the March 1978 raid near Tel Aviv, which resulted in dead and 76 wounded Israelis. In response, the Isra forces invaded Lebanon on the night of 14/15 Mar occupying the entire region south of the Litani Riv except for the city of Tyre, within a few days.

On 15 March the Lebanese government submit a protest against the Israeli invasion to the Secur Council, stating that Lebanon had no connection w the Palestinian presence and commando operatio They further argued that they had attempted to br the border regions under ADF control, but had be

A Finnish XA-180 Sisu armoured vehicle attac to UNDOF on patrol al the Golan Heights, December 1990. (Unitec Nations/J. Isaac)

peded by the Israelis and their insistence on aintenance of the 'red line' troop demarcation leaving em powerless to intervene. On 19 March, in a oposal by the United States, the Security Council opted Resolutions 425 (1978) and 436 (1978), which lled for the immediate cessation of military action and thdrawal of Israeli forces from Lebanese territory, d the establishment of a United Nations Interim orce for Lebanon (UNIFIL) for a period of six months subject to extension, with an authorized strength of 7,000.

UNIFIL was established with the mandate of confirming the Israeli withdrawal from southern Lebanon, the restoration of peace and security, and assisting in the establishment of the authority of the Lebanese government in the area. UNIFIL operations are centred on static Southern Lebanese positions manned 24 hours a day, including 45 checkpoints that control movement

Above: Norwegian UNIFIL troops search for mines in Southern Lebanon, November 1990. They wear green and woodland-camouflage US PASGT armour vests over green fatigues. (United Nations/J. Isaac)

NIFIL jacket insignia: e 13cm diameter disc, rdered in blue wool with vhite cotton twill centre, atures the UN global ojection and coloured gs of countries of the rce, with outlines, eath, and lettering in ld bullion. (Author's oto)

Nepalese UNIFIL ldier on guard duty at a uthern Lebanon sition, April 1978. The palese Battalion is ployed in the central d eastern sectors, nning 11 positions. Of erest is the hand-broidered 'Nepal' tab d UN shoulder sleeve ignia fixed to the man's sey with safety pins. nited Nations/J. Isaac)

on the main thoroughfares in the area, 95 observation posts that monitor road travel, and 29 checkpoints/ observation posts. Through continued observation and foot and vehicle patrols each position ensures that hostile activities are not undertaken, while providing the local population with protection, and medical and humanitarian assistance. Unarmed military observers of the UN Truce Supervision Organization (UNTSO), under UNIFIL command, man five observation posts and operate five mobile observation teams in Israeli-controlled areas. UNIFIL was prevented from deploying to the area evacuated by the Israelis between April and June 1978. This border enclave was turned over to the Israeli-supported Christian militias, thus retaining Israeli control and guaranteeing continued fighting against the PLO.

In June 1982 Israel invaded Lebanon for a second time, with a partial withdrawal in 1985 and retained military control over the southern border area aided by the South Lebanon Army. Any PLO attacks provoked an Israeli response with heavy weapons and air attacks.

From its inception UNIFIL has been unable to fu... its mandate due to a lack of co-operation and continu... harassment from both the PLO and the Government... Israel, while taking numerous casualties (170 fatalities... of June 1990).

United Nations Transition Assistance Group (UNTAG)

Germany annexed the Territory of South West Afri... now Namibia, in 1884, retaining control of the area un... the First World War, when a South African invasion... July 1915 defeated the German forces. In Decemb... 1920 the League of Nations conferred upon the Sou... African Government a mandate to administer Sou... West Africa. After the Second World War the Unit... Nations assumed the League's responsibilities; a... South Africa sought to incorporate the region as a fi... province, while granting whites living in the territo... direct representation in the South African parliame... The International Court of Justice (ICJ), at the requ... of the General Assembly, gave numerous advis... opinions on the situation, including a 1950 conclusi... that South Africa held no legal obligation to conclud... trustee agreement with the UN and that the mandate w... still in force.

In 1962 Ethiopia and Liberia, the only African sta... that had been members of the League of Natio... brought suit against South Africa, alleging that int... national obligations had not been met, as South Afr... implemented the Odendaal Report dividing the regi... into 12 homelands largely under white control. In J... 1966 the South West African People's Organizat... (SWAPO), with Angolan, Cuban, and Soviet-b... assistance, initiated a guerrilla war against South Afric... rule. In October 1966 the General Assembly pass... Resolution 2145 revoking the South African mand... over the territory; and in 1970 passed Resolution 2... stating that South Africa's presence in the region v... illegal. In 1971 the ICJ confirmed the revocation of t... mandate and declared that South Africa must withdr... and end occupation of the territory.

In 1975 South Africa convened a constitutional co... ference in Windhoek with the Odendaal homeland lea... ers. This conference established an interim governm... with the stated aim of establishing independence... South West Africa in late 1976. On 30 January 19...

A Finnish member of UNTAG in Rundu near the Angolan Border, April 1989. A total of 863 Finnish troops were deployed in north-eastern Namibia near the Angolan, Zambian, and Botswana borders. Along with Keny... and Malaysia, Finland w... one of three among 50 participating countries t... contribute complete unit... of infantry to UNTAG. (United Nations/M. Gra...

*s part of the United
ations Transition
ssistance Group
JNTAG) in Namibia,
nnish peace-keeping
rces arrive in
rootfontein aboard a US
ir Force C-5A Galaxy
ansport, April 1989.
hough the US has
ployed few ground
oops to UN missions
nder UN command (the
orean and Gulf Wars,
d early Somalia mission
ere predominantly US
erations), they have
ntributed airlift of
oops and supplies and
gistics support to
merous missions.
Jnited Nations/M.
rant)*

solution 385, declaring the need for free elections in
e region, was adopted, but subsequently ignored by the
uth Africans. On 10 April 1978 a new proposal for the
ttlement of the Namibian situation was put forward.
his comprised all elements of Resolution 385 but pro-
sed a compromise that allowed South Africa to admin-
er elections under UN supervision assisted by a United
ations Transition Assistance Group (UNTAG). The
oposal outlined a timetable for action by various
oups, a cease-fire in the war between South Africa and
VAPO, the dismantling and demobilization of the local
litary force (South West Africa Territorial Force and
lice) and its command structure, the release of political
isoners, the unobstructed return of all Namibian refu-
es to participate in free and fair elections, and the
aceful return of SWAPO forces through UN super-
ed entry points. On 29 September 1978 the Security
uncil adopted Resolution 435, which established the
finite plan for Namibian independence incorporating
ny provisions of the proposal, modifying the timetable,
d outlining the resources needed to complete the plan.
fore implementation of Resolution 435 numerous con-
tations took place, and a regional settlement was
ached involving the United States, the Soviet Union,
uth Africa, SWAPO, and Cuba.

UNTAG, mainly a political organisation to ensure
e and fair elections, was required to carry out
merous tasks, many of which were unlike tasks
rformed by previous peace-keeping operations. These
luded monitoring the cease-fire, reduction and re-
val of South African forces from the area, ensuring
t the South West African Police and security forces

carried out their duties consistently with free and fair
elections, and ensuring that a change in the political
climate took place to enable the population to feel free
from intimidation. At the maximum deployment, from 7
to 11 November 1989, UNTAG consisted of over 2,000
civilians, 1,500 police monitors, and 4,500 military
personnel. The election process, by secret ballot and
open to every Namibian, was monitored by the UN
Special Representative, who guaranteed the fairness of
the elections and prepared all aspects of the electoral
process.

The high visibility, strict timetable for completion,
and logistical problems, made UNTAG the most
demanding operation that the UN had undertaken at that
time. Though revolutionary, and beyond the traditional
peace-keeping role, UNTAG was a bright spot in the
history of UN peace-keeping and a model of co-
operation among the 50 nations taking part in the
mission to ensure the independence of Namibia.

The Gulf War 1991

The Emirate of Kuwait was granted independence from
the United Kingdom in 1961. The Iraqi leader at that
time, General Qasim, refused recognition of the state and
proclaimed Kuwait to be a part of Iraq. Kuwait was
given membership in the League of Arab States in 1961
and in the United Nations in 1963. On 2 August 1990
Iraqi forces invaded and occupied the State of Kuwait,
President Saddam Hussein's regime declaring it the 19th
Province of Iraq. The UN Security Council demanded
an immediate and unconditional withdrawal of Iraqi
forces from Kuwaiti soil, and on 4 August instituted

A soldier of 1st Battalion US 325th Airborne Infantry Regiment stands by as a Saudi Arabian National Guardsman shoulders an FIM-92A Stinger anti-aircraft missile launcher. The US soldier wears the ubiquitous six-colour desert BDU, PASGT helmet with cloth cover, and green ALICE gear. The Saudi corporal, or Arif, wears a two-colour (brown and khaki) camouflage uniform with a black stripe of rank embroidered on camouflage material on the left arm, and a British helmet. (US Army/S. Henry)

British soldiers from 1st The Queen's Dragoon Guards and US Marines from 7th Platoon, 1st Force Reconnaissance Company watch as a British soldier fires a US M-40A1 sniper rifle during weapons training at the Abu Hydra Range, Saudi Arabia. The British troops wear the two-colour desert camouflage uniform, armour vest, and bush hat. (US Marine Corps/J.R. Ruark)

economic sanctions against Iraq. Allied member states co-operating with the Kuwaiti government were authorized by Resolution 678 (29 November 1990) to use all means necessary to uphold the Security Council's resolutions and to restore peace and security to the region. Without any stand-by military forces, the UN delegated the enforcement of Security Council resolutions to the nations (later known as the Coalition Forces) allied with Kuwait and commanded by the United States. A deadline of 15 January 1991 was established for Iraq to co-operate with the UN. The deadline passed and the next day the Coalition Forces began massive air attacks against the Iraqi forces, followed on 24 February by a ground assault. By 27 February the Iraqi forces were fleeing Kuwait and hostilities were suspended.

On 3 April 1991, while maintaining economic

embers of the 500-strong [N]iger Army contingent to [th]e Multi-National Force [du]ring an inspection. All [we]ar six-colour daytime [de]sert BDUs, US M1 [he]lmets with the brown *side of the 1960s cover showing, US M17A1 gas masks, and green US-type web gear. Note the US M-14 rifles equipped with bipods. (US Air Force/H. Deffner)*

[sa]nctions against Iraq, Security Council Resolution 687 [es]tablished conditions for the cease-fire and its supervi[si]on. These conditions have been referred to as 'the [m]other of all resolutions' and include the demarcation of [th]e 1963 Iraq-Kuwait border; a UN observer unit [(U]NIKOM) to be stationed on the border; the destruc[tio]n of all Iraqi chemical, biological, and nuclear weapons [an]d ballistic missiles with a range greater than 150 [kil]ometres as well as on-site inspection of these weapons; [Ira]qi liability for any loss, damage, or injury as a result of [the] occupation of Kuwait; and acceptance of the [co]ntinuation of economic sanctions. Iraq accepted Reso[lu]tion 687, but under protest, claiming it was illegal and [un]just. On 3 April 1991 (by Resolution 687) a [de]militarized zone (DMZ) was established along the lines [of] the 1963 Iraq-Kuwait border extending five kilometres [int]o Kuwait and ten kilometres into Iraq. The UN Iraq-[Ku]wait Observation Mission (UNIKOM) was estab[lis]hed to monitor the DMZ and the Khawr' Abd Allah

waterway. The final cease-fire came into effect on 12 April.

After the Gulf War, with Saddam Hussein still in power, Iraq brutally crushed Kurdish rebellions in the north and Shi'ite revolts in the south of the country. On 10 April 1991 President Bush ordered all military activity to cease north of the 36th Parallel. A safe haven for Kurds was later created in the north.

United Nations Iraq-Kuwait Observation Mission (UNIKOM)

The 3 April 1991 adoption of Security Council Resolution 687 established elaborate conditions for the cease-fire between the Coalition Forces and the Republic of Iraq after the Gulf War. These included: UN monitoring of a 200-kilometre-long demilitarized zone (DMZ) along the boundary of Iraq and Kuwait, extending ten kilometres into Iraq and five kilometres into Kuwait; monitoring the 40-kilometre Khawr'Abd Allah waterway between Iraq and Kuwait and the DMZ; deterring violations of the boundary; and observing any hostile actions. Resolution 689 (9 April 1991), formally approving the establishment of the United Nations Iraq-Kuwait Observation Mission (UNIKOM) with an authorized strength of 686, stated that the mission could only be

An honour guard from the French Foreign Legion's 6th Foreign Engineer Battalion stand at attention as they await the arrival of Lt.Gen. Aziz, commander of Joint Forces in Saudi Arabia, during Operation 'Desert Shield'. All wear the Satin 300 uniform with the Legion's red and green epaulettes and white kepi and carry the 5.56mm FAMAS rifle. (US Air Force/H. Deffner)

terminated by a Security Council decision, not by request from one of the host countries as had been standard practice in earlier peace-keeping operations; and that the US-led Coalition Nations each have veto power to prevent the withdrawal of UNIKOM. The UNIKOM mandate was set for a six-month period and has been reinstated continuously at six-month intervals.

An advance party of UNIKOM under the command of Maj.Gen. Gunther Greindl (Austria), formerly the UNFICYP force commander in Cyprus, arrived in the area on 13 April 1991. Units from UNFICYP and UNIFIL in Lebanon arrived on 15 April and full deployment was achieved by 6 May. A temporary headquarters was established at the SAS Hotel in Kuwait City (later to be moved to a permanent site at Umm Qasr in the Iraqi zone of the DMZ on 1 November). After monitoring the withdrawal of troops still in the area the military presence of the Coalition Forces in Iraq was terminated, and the DMZ was established on 9 May in accordance with Resolution 686. By late September 1992 UNIKOM strength was reduced from 1,385 to 599 as threats of Iraqi action failed to materialize.

UNIKOM conducts ground and air patrols, maintains static observation points, and employs investigation and liaison teams to verify that no military personnel, equipment, or military installations are maintained in the DMZ. For operational purposes the DMZ is divided into three sectors, with a headquarters and six observation points/patrol bases per sector. Observers patrol their area of operations while visiting temporary observation points established in areas with road networks or high activity. The Khawr'Abd Allah waterway is patrolled by helicopter or fixed-wing aircraft, as are areas of the DMZ where mines endanger the safety of ground patrols. Other UNIKOM activities include the disposal of mines and other unexploded ordnance, by mid-1992 1,400 kilometres of track had been cleared and 14,000 mines disposed of.

UNIKOM military observers are unarmed, authorized to use force only in self-defence, and have no authority or means to prevent the entry of military personnel or equipment into the DMZ. Maintenance of law and order is the responsibility of the governments of Kuwait and Iraq and each polices their own zone. From an operational point of view UNIKOM is independent from other UN Iraq-Kuwait missions, though other missions have requested UNIKOM support. The Iraq-Kuwait Boundary Demarcation Commission has requested UNIKOM support for mine demolition, the placing of survey markers, transport, and security. The UN Return of Property from Iraq to Kuwait Mission requested UNIKOM security and escort for returned supplies, boats, and helicopters from Iraq.

The UNIKOM mission, for the first time in the history of UN peace-keeping, consisted of military observers and other personnel drawn from all five permanent members of the Security Council, with the participation of the first UN Chinese contingent.

The unarmed UNIKOM mission is limited in scope and has been unable to prevent numerous Iraqi incursions into Kuwait, the largest violation being a 1993 raid at Umm Qasr when 250 Iraqis crossed the border and confiscated 12 Chinese-manufactured Silkworm missiles that were scheduled for demolition, at a former

aqi base. An elaborate series of trenches, berms, and
ectronic surveillance equipment is now under construc-
on by the Kuwaitis along the border, and this will
cilitate the UNIKOM mission in the future.

*bove: A US Marine
*ficer assigned to
*NIKOM entering the
*rret of a LAV, 1992. He
*ears the standard UN
*'ue beret with metal
*dge and three-colour
*aytime desert BDUs.
*Marine Corps Historical
ollection)

*he United Nations
*bserver Mission in El
*alvador (ONUSAL)
*olice contingent provide
*aining to that country's
*ational Police Force.
*ere Mexican (second
*om left) and Spanish
*econd from right) police
*sist a Salvadorean police
*ficer (far right) during a
*utine traffic stop,
*bruary 1992. (United
ations/J. Bleibtreu)

United Nations Observer Mission in El Salvador (ONUSAL)

In 1981 President Ronald Reagan drew the line against
Communism in El Salvador 18 months after the fall of
Nicaragua to the Sandinistas. Amid allegations of Soviet
and Cuban military aid funnelled through Nicaragua to
the anti-government Frente Farabundo Marti para la
Liberacion Nacional (FMLN)[1] a massive US effort
began to equip and modernize the Salvadoran Army in
their fight against the FMLN. After ten years of US aid,
deployment of US Special Forces trainers, an estimated
70,000 casualties, numerous extreme human rights
abuses, the murder of foreigners by right-wing death
squads, and a failed FMLN final offensive, the military
situation reached a stalemate.

In an effort to resolve the hostilities by political
means negotiations were initiated in September 1989
between the Government of El Salvador and the FMLN,
and conducted under the auspices of the UN Secretary-
General. The objectives of the negotiations were to end
armed conflict, promote democracy in the region,
guarantee respect for human rights, and reunite Salvadoran society. On 26 July 1990 the first agreement on
human rights was signed by both parties at San Jose,
Costa Rica; this provided for the establishment of a UN
mission to monitor the progress of freedom in the area.
Security Council Resolution 693 of 20 May 1991
established the United Nations Observer Mission in El

(1) The FMLN is a coalition of groups established to counter 50 years of Salvadoran military
and land owner rule.

With the goal of peace not only for El Salvador but for the entire region, the United Nations Observer Group in Central America (ONUCA) was formed. Here Venezuelan contingent members destroy a surrendered Contra AK-47 at La Kiatara-Moquitia, Honduras, April 1990. (United Nations/S. Johansen)

Salvador (ONUSAL), with an authorized strength of 1,146, as a peace-keeping/peace-making operation with a mandate to monitor the human rights situation, to investigate specific violations, to promote human rights, and to make recommendations for the elimination of violations. From July through September 1991 ONUSAL established a presence and set up offices in the country. By 1 October the investigation of human rights violations had begun, with the goal of establishing the validity of claims identifying and punishing guilty parties and determing future violations.

Additional progress was made at the negotiating table and an agreement to end the armed struggle was signed on 31 December 1991 (The Act of New York). With negotiations on all major issues completed, the final peace agreement was signed in Mexico City on 16 January 1992. ONUSAL's mandate now included verification of the cease-fire, separation of forces, and maintenance of public order while a National Civil Police was established. Three ONUSAL divisions were established to monitor the human rights, military, and police situations in the country. The Human Rights Division, as established under Resolution 693, was responsible for verifying the implementation of the Human Rights Agreement and consisted of 40 observers, legal advisers, and educators. The Military Division, established on 20 January 1992 with a strength of 380 military observers, was responsible for verifying the redeployment of the El Salvador military forces to peacetime positions and the concentration of FMLN forces to designated areas, while verifying weapons and personnel, and investigating violations on both sides. The Police Division, consisting of international civil police specialists, monitored National Police activities, and supervised and trained the police in preparation for the establishment of a new National Civil Police.

It is anticipated that the ONUSAL mission will be completed with the monitoring of general elections scheduled for March 1994.

THE BALKANS

The roots of the conflict in the Balkans can be traced the 11th century when Balkan Christians split into two culturally and religiously antagonistic societies. The western Catholic Croats followed the Pope in Rome while the eastern Serbs were loyal to the Orthodox church in Constantinople. In the 14th century the Balkans were partitioned by the Ottoman Turks when Prince Lauch was defeated at the battle of Kosovo condemning much of the region to 500 years of Turkish rule and the partial introduction of the Islamic faith. The centuries which followed were fertile ground for a web tangled resentments, alliances, and deeply implanted hatred which persists to this day.

Yugoslavia was formed on 4 December 1918 from the Balkan states and territories formerly under Turkish and latterly Austro-Hungarian rule. King Peter I Serbia reigned until his son Alexander I succeeded him in 1929. Croatian demands provoked Alexander assume dictatorial powers amid widespread resentment

1934 the first attempt at unification was made by ing Alexander, who was assassinated by Croatian rorists resisting perceived domination by the Serbs.

The Second World War perpetuated deep-rooted utual fears and hatreds, with a Nazi puppet state tablished in Croatia (including most of Bosnia). These roatian fascists, or Ustasha, together with some Muslim ies, adopted strict racial laws, and enthusiastically rsecuted Serbs, Jews, and gypsies with the goal of oducing an 'ethnically clean' territory: it is estimated at some 500,000 Serbs were killed, often with medieval uelty, in the process. The Utashas were fought by the onarchist Chetniks, and the Soviet-leaning Partisans der Josip Broz Tito.

Tito won a form of election in 1945; limiting mass venge for fascist war crimes to a brief and fairly ntrolled period of summary savagery, he divided the untry into the provinces of Slovenia, Croatia, Bosnia-ercegovina and Macedonia, and the two autonomous gions of Vojvodina and Kosovo. This action was seen the Serbs as a denial of their victory over the Nazis, d as a loss of territory (Kosovo, Macedonia, and ojvodina were traditionally Serbian-dominated) which inforced their resentment. Tito broke ties with the oviet bloc in 1948 and followed a middle road.

For 35 years Tito's regime curbed ethnic and ligious tensions; but hostilities resurfaced after his ath in May 1980, aggravated by the worsening onomy. In 1989 the Serbs, long dominant in the vernment and armed forces of Yugoslavia, engineered creased authority over Kosovo. Though traditionally nsidered the cradle of Serbian culture Kosovo's opulation now comprised 90% Albanian Muslims. The pression of the population which followed helped flame feelings in the rest of the country but made a cal hero of the Serbian leader Slobodan Milosevic. In ne 1991 Slovenia and Croatia declared independence, ompting almost immediate attacks from the Serbian-d Yugoslav Army. In Croatia President Tujman itiated policies which aggravated resentment between e Croats and Serbs, using television propaganda to stir hatred and polarize political support. Croatian tremists rewrote history to down-play the country's llaboration with the Nazis, purged the police of rbian officers, excluded Serbs from Croatian citizen-ip, and declared independence from Yugoslavia. The rbs, who have traditionally seen themselves as his-rical victims refused to accept mediation, and un-shed the so-called Yugoslav People's Army. In

February 1992 Bosnia-Herzegovina voted for indepen-dence, prompting Serb irregulars, supported by the Yugoslav Army, to attack Bosnian Muslims and Croats. In April 1992 Serbia and Montenegro declared a new Yugoslav Republic, while Yugoslav Army troops with-drew from Macedonia.

UNPROFOR in Croatia

The UN became actively involved in the crisis in the Balkans (former Yugoslav Republics) on 25 September 1991, when the Security Council adopted Resolution 713 implementing an embargo on the shipment of military weapons to Yugoslavia. The UN appointed Mr Cyrus Vance as the Secretary-General's personal envoy for Yugoslavia; he negotiated with the Presidents of Serbia and Croatia, and reached an agreement that led to a series of cease-fires (which were almost immediately broken) and to agreement on the establishment of a UN peace-keeping operation. On 21 February 1992 Security Council Resolution 743 established the creation of the United Nations Protection Force (UNPROFOR) in Croatia for a period of 12 months subject to review. UNPROFOR was deployed in three UN Protected Areas (UNPAs) in Croatia: Eastern Slavonia, Western Slavonia, and Krajina, where Serbs make up a majority

NPROFOR Danish ttalion members at eir headquarters in *Kostajnica, Croatia, September 1992. (United Nations/J. Isaac)*

and conflicts have historically erupted. UNPROFOR's mandate was to ensure the demilitarization of the UNPAs, to protect all civilians in those areas, to assist in the return of refugees to their homes, to monitor the functions of the local police, and to support the work of UN humanitarian agencies. In June 1992 UNPROFOR's mandate was enlarged to include monitoring areas (so-called 'pink zones') within the Yugoslav National Army lines and populated by Serbs, to perform immigration and custom functions at the UNPA international borders, monitor the demilitarization of the Prevlaka Peninsula and control the Peruca Dam.

UNPROFOR in Bosnia-Herzegovina

The situation in Bosnia-Herzegovina (Bosnia) deteriorated to the point where in April 1992 the UN passed a series of resolutions calling for a cease-fire: the cessation of interference from the Yugoslav People's Army and Croatian Army in Bosnia; and for the disbandment of local irregular forces. On 30 May Security Council Resolution 757 imposed wide-ranging sanctions on Yugoslavia (then consisting of Serbia and Montenegro), the establishment of a security zone at Sarajevo Airport, and conditions for the unimpeded delivery of humanitarian supplies in the region. On 5 June an agreement was negotiated with the Bosnian Serbs for UNPROFOR to take control of Sarajevo Airport in order to reopen it for humanitarian purposes; Security Council Resolution 761 was passed, authorizing deployment of UNPROFOR to

Above: Kenyan Battalion members at UNPROFOR Headquarters, Zagreb, Croatia, 1993. Both wear the Kenyan version of temperate DPM camouflage with UN shoulder sleeve insignia fixed to tan brassards. Note the KENBATT insignia on the rear of the Land-Rover. (W.E. Storey Collection)

United Nations Protection Force (UNPROFOR) Canadian contingent members showing UN Under-Secretary-General Goulding (third from right) and UNPROFOR commander Lt.Gen. Nambiar (far left) a collection of land mines unearthed in the area surrounding Daruvar, eastern Croatia, September 1992. (United Nations/J. Isaac)

A UNPROFOR Danish battalion member calibrating a night viewing device in Kostajnica, Croatia, September 1992. The red and white Danish tab and insignia can be seen on the left shoulder (United Nations/J. Isaac)

UN peace-keepers undergoing communications training in the field by a Finnish warrant officer (far right), a member of FINCOY/NORDBAT/UNPROFOR. (Finnish Ministry of Defense)

the airport. Though there was continued fighting in the area the airport was reopened for humanitarian purposes on 3 July.

On 10 September UNPROFOR's mandate was extended to support efforts by the UN High Commissioner for Refugees and to provide security for humanitarian aid shipments throughout Bosnia, as well as protecting convoys of civilians under the protection of the International Committee of the Red Cross. UNPROFOR was deployed in four zones, each deployment consisting of one infantry battalion with civilian and liaison support, under normal peace-keeping rules of engagement authorized to use force only in self-defence. On 9 October Security Council Resolution 781 banned all military flights over Bosnia (except for UNPROFOR, other UN, or humanitarian flights). UNPROFOR was instructed to monitor compliance with the ban and established observation posts at airfields in the Bosnia, Croatia, and Yugoslavia. On 21 December UNPROFOR's mandate was again enlarged to include the right to search for and confiscate military weapons, or other sanctioned goods, smuggled into Bosnia. These new duties were to be conducted by a full-time observation and search operation located at 123 border points.

UNPROFOR in Macedonia

On 11 November 1992 the President of Macedonia, voicing concern about the impact of fighting in the former Yugoslav republics and the effect upon his newly created country, requested the preventive deployment of a UN observer group to Macedonia. By Security Council Resolution 795 of 11 December 1992 UNPROFOR's mandate was enlarged to establish a presence on Macedonia's borders with Albania, Serbia, and Kosovo in order to monitor and report developments in the border areas that might prove a security threat to Macedonia. A Macedonia Command was established with headquarters in Skopje, the capital of Macedonia, consisting of one battalion of up to 700 all ranks, 26 civilian staff members, 10 civil affairs officers, 35 military observers, and 45 administrative staff and interpreters. This brought total UNPROFOR strength in Croatia, Bosnia, and Macedonia to over 23,000.

For the first time US armed forces were placed under UN command, and deployed to Macedonia on 6 July 1993 as part of UNPROFOR. Three hundred members of the Berlin Brigade were airlifted into Macedonia to train and operate alongside UN Scandinavian forces of NORDBAT.

At the time of writing there have been innumerable cynically agreed and broken cease-fires, failed partition plans, half-hearted threats of direct military action by Western powers, and continued civilian suffering, especially in Sarajevo and other areas of Bosnia. The essential characteristic of this operation is that UN forces are powerless to achieve more than temporary and local humanitarian aid in a situation where all the warring parties are still determined to try to improve their position by continued fighting.

CAMBODIA

Another chapter in the long Cambodian nightmare ended on 23 October 1991 with the last UN-sponsored meeting of the Paris Conference on Cambodia. The Paris Agreement and Security Council Resolutions 718 (31 October 1991) and 745 (19 February 1992) established the United Nations Transitional Authority in Cambodia (UNTAC), mandated to conduct free and fair elections, military arrangements, civil administration, maintenance of law and order, resettlement of refugees, and rebuilding of the country's infrastructure until the Supreme

National Council of Cambodia (SNC), consisting of fo Cambodian factions[2], had approved a constitution a created a new government. UNTAC became operatio on 15 March 1992, and started disarming and d mobilization (known as Phase II) of the belligerents on May.

From the start the PDK (Khmer Rouge) failed co-operate, refusing UNTAC entry into its area operation and failing to disclose troop strengths agreed to in the Paris Agreement. Negotiations co ducted by Thailand and Japan failed to persuade t PDK to comply with the provisions of the Pa Agreement; with numerous cease-fire violations a increased attacks upon UN forces, the disarmament a demobilization process was halted. On 30 Novemb UNTAC, in response to Security Council Resoluti 792, established border checkpoints in order to veri the withdrawal and non-return of foreign forces and t halt of outside military assistance to the belligeren and to prevent the supply of fuels reaching any facti that did not comply with the terms of the Pa Agreement. Though Phase II of the cease-fire w halted, other aspects of the UNTAC mandate we successful, including the human rights, elector military, civil administrative, civilian police, repatri tion, and rehabilitation components.

The UNTAC human rights component, responsib for developing an atmosphere of respect for hum rights, in which free and fair elections could take plac reviewed the Cambodian judicial and legal systems light of international provisions, conducted an extensi human rights education campaign, investigated hum rights-related complaints, and took corrective acti where necessary. On 20 April the SNC ratified nume ous international human rights covenants and conve tions.

The UNTAC electoral component, responsible conducting free and fair elections no later than M 1993, designed and implemented systems for each pha of the electoral process (with the SNC). This began wi a framework of electoral law and regulations governi the electoral process and a code of conduct. UNTA also participated in voter training and education, vot registration of over 4.6 million Cambodians within thr months, and overseeing the polling process at bo mobile and fixed polling stations.

The UNTAC military component was responsib for verification of the withdrawal of foreign forces fro

(2) These factions include: the Party of the State of Cambodia (SOC); the Khmer Peop National Liberation Front (KPNLF); the United Front for an Independent, Neutral, Peac and Cooperative Cambodia (FUNCINPEC); and the Party of Democratic Kampuchea (PD or Khmer Rouge.

On 29 May 1992, 470 French soldiers from the APRONUC (Autorité Provisoire des Nations Unies au Cambodge /UN Provisional Authority in Cambodia) Battalion were deployed to Cambodia as part of the United Nations Transitional Authority in Cambodia (UNTAC).

They were deployed in Zone 2 along the Laotian border, and Zone 6 along a 350km line on the border from Thailand to Vietnam. Here French troops stand inspection in Phnom Penh, October 1992. (United Nations/P. Sudhakaran)

[m]bodia; supervision of the cease-fire, this included [re]groupment, disarming, demobilization, weapons con[tro]l, and locating and confiscating weapons caches; [as]sisting in mine clearance and training; investigation of [no]n-compliance with any arrangements; and assistance in [th]e release of prisoners and in the repatriation of [re]fugees. These tasks were accomplished by the estab[lis]hment of checkpoints located in airports, sea ports, on [ma]jor roads, and along Cambodia's borders. By the [ce]ssation of Phase II of the cease-fire, due to the lack of [co]-operation from the PDK, 55,000 troops of the [Ca]mbodian factions had been demobilized out of a total [of] 200,000 regular and 250,000 militia forces.

The UNTAC civil administrative component, [re]sponsible for establishing an atmosphere conducive to [fre]e and fair elections, had set up offices in all [Ca]mbodian provinces by 1 July 1992, and concentrated [th]eir efforts on five key areas of the administration: [fo]reign affairs, national defence, public safety, finance [an]d information.

The UNTAC civilian police component was respon[sib]le for the supervision of the local police, ensuring that [la]w and order was maintained effectively and impartially [an]d that human rights were observed. By December [19]92 the police component reached full deployment and [pr]ovided training in basic police procedures and traffic [co]ntrol, implementation of a new penal code, and [as]sisted the military component in supervising the [ch]eckpoints.

A UNTAC Bangladesh [co]ntingent member of the [U]N Mine Clearance Unit [in]structing a Cambodian [ar]my soldier in the use of [th]e mine detector, 1992. It

was estimated that 4.5 million mines were laid throughout the country during its long years of conflict. (United Nations/ J. Bleibtreu)

An UNTAC French paratrooper examining a folding-stock AK-47 belonging to a Khmer Rouge soldier, July 1992. The French mission was supposedly to disarm the warring forces (6,000 in Zone 6 alone); this was to be accomplished by 30 paras stationed at each disarming point. (United Nations/J. Bleibtreu)

The UNTAC repatriation component was responsible for the repatriation of over 300,000 refugees and displaced persons to Cambodia from March 1992 to April 1993. The UN Development Program assisted with the provision of health care, education, water and agriculture, as well as improving the infrastructure for the returnees.

The UNTAC rehabilitation component provided food, security, health, housing, training and education, and restoration of the basic infrastructure. By January 1993 42 projects were in process and $880 million in aid was pledged by the international community.

The United Nations Transitional Authority in Cambodia has been one of the largest and most costly missions undertaken to date, with over 22,000 military and civilian personnel involved and a cost of over $3 billion (with refugee repatriation and resettlement costs funded by additional voluntary contributions). The UNTAC peace-making, peace-keeping, and peace-building mission was a relative success; but with the PDK's refusal to disarm, there is a danger that the country could be plunged back into civil war in the future.

SOMALIA

The overthrow of President Siad Barre in January 1991 resulted in a power struggle between traditional and clan-based factions throughout Somalia. Intense fighting broke out in Mogadishu, the capital, between the factions of Interim President Ali Mahdi Mohammed, and that of General Mohammed Farah Aidid and his United Somali Congress; hostilities quickly spread throughout the country. The fighting caused almost one million Somalis to seek refuge in neighbouring countries, and widespread famine and disease which claimed an estimated 300,000 civilian lives in the first 18 months of the conflict. With another 1.5 million lives at risk due to lack of food, political chaos, widespread looting hampering the delivery of humanitarian aid and placing UN and Red Cross workers' lives in danger, and the threat to stability of neighbouring countries, the Secretary General, in cooperation with the Organization of African Unity (OAU), the League of Arab States (LAS), and the Organization of the Islamic Conference (OIC), pressed for a peaceful resolution to the conflict.

In January 1992 a team of senior UN officials led by Under Secretary-General for Political Affairs James O. Jonah travelled to Somalia to facilitate an end to the fighting. Support for a cease-fire was agreed to by all factions except that of General Aidid. In response to the agreement in principle, the UN (by Resolution 733, January 1992) established a complete embargo on military goods to Somalia, an increase in humanitarian aid, the promotion of a cease-fire, and assistance in a political settlement. A UN-sponsored meeting held on January in New York attended by representatives of the LAS, OAU, OIC and the two main warring factions succeeded in an agreement on a cease-fire that was signed in Mogadishu on 3 March. This agreement also provided for a UN security component for humanitarian supplies, the deployment of UN observers to monitor each faction, and the establishment of a national reconciliation

nference that all Somali factions would attend (adopted
17 March 1991 as Security Council Resolution 746).
24 April the Security Council adopted Resolution
1, establishing the United Nations Operation in
malia (UNOSOM).

A group of 50 UN observers arrived in Mogadishu
early July 1992, with the deployment of an additional
0 UN security personnel on 14 September 1992. The
N was prevented from distributing humanitarian
pplies due to looting by heavily armed groups and
acks on ships and at airports. On 28 August an
crease in UNOSOM strength by four security units of
0 men each was approved by Resolution 775. In
tober 1992 the situation deteriorated to the point
ere rival militias divided the capital between them,
ile 12 or more factions roamed the countryside looting
manitarian supplies, and engaging in kidnapping,
bbery, extortion, and other acts of banditry.
NOSOM troops were fired upon and UN vehicles and

low: Belgian members
the Unified Task Force
NITAF), which
linquished operational
thority to UNOSOM in
rly May 1993, at
smayo airfield, April
93. (United Nations/M.
ant)

Right: Armoured vehicles
of the Nigerian contingent
to the United Nations
Operations in Somalia
(UNOSOM) in Mogadishu,
May 1993. (United
Nations/M. Grant)

arms seized, while relief ships were blocked from docking and shelled resulting in only a small amount of relief supplies reaching the needy in the countryside. It was estimated that as many as 3,000 people per day were dying of starvation while warehouses remained full.

Television newscasts showed the plight of the Somalian people in ever more emotional terms, and public opinion led the Bush Administration to offer United States leadership in organizing and commanding an international rescue of the Somali people by an operation to ensure the delivery of relief supplies. Under Resolution 794 (3 December 1992) the use of all necessary means to establish a secure environment for the delivery of relief supplies was mandated. In response, the United States spearheaded a Unified Task Force (UNITAF), Operation 'Restore Hope', which deployed to Mogadishu on 9 December 1992 amid massive media attention.

In Phase I of the deployment, the Mogadishu port facilities and the airfields at Bale Dogle and Baidoa were secured by 16 December. Phase II saw part of eight relief centres (Kismayo, Bardera, Oddur, Gialalassi, and Belet Huen) secured on 28 December, and the landing of elements of the US 10th Mountain Division; while Phase III secured the additional relief centres and Kismayo airport and port, and the continuation of relief operations. UNITAF, a five-month operation with 18 Task Force deaths, established a secure environment for

delivery of humanitarian aid shipments, and turned ov military command (Phase IV) to the UN and UNOSO in May 1993.

The mood of welcome among Somalis soon sour as UNOSOM took command, and attacks agai UNOSOM accelerated, culminating in the 5 Ju ambush near Mogadishu's October 21st Road which l 24 dead, 40 wounded, and five captured Pakistani pea keepers. In response the UN passed Resolution 8 calling for the punishment of those responsible for t killings, believed to be General Aidid and his Unit Somali Congress. On 12 June a pre-dawn punitive str on General Aidid's residence and other sites throughо Mogadishu was undertaken, this involved both grou forces and a US Air Force AC-130H Spectre gunsh (one of four gunships eventually deployed to the are On 17 June the UN officially called for the arrest General Aidid. The game of cat-and-mouse continu with the US dispatching Ranger units and elements the anti-terrorist Delta Force to the region in August attempt the capture of General Aidid; these attemp failed. Casualties mounted on both sides, culminating the 3 October downing of two US helicopters; in t ensuing confused fighting 78 US servicemen we wounded, one captured, and 15 killed, while as many 300 Somalis (including civilians) lost their lives. This о incident caused the UN and US to reconsider th mission; and ultimately resulted in the resignation of t US Secretary of Defense, Les Aspin, in December 19

Members of the Botswar contingent to UNOSOM on inspection at Camp Higgins (named in hono of US Col. William Higgins who was abduc and killed while serving a peace-keeper in Lebanon). The Botswanans wear their recently adopted DPM camouflage uniforms; Bardera, April 1993. (United Nations)

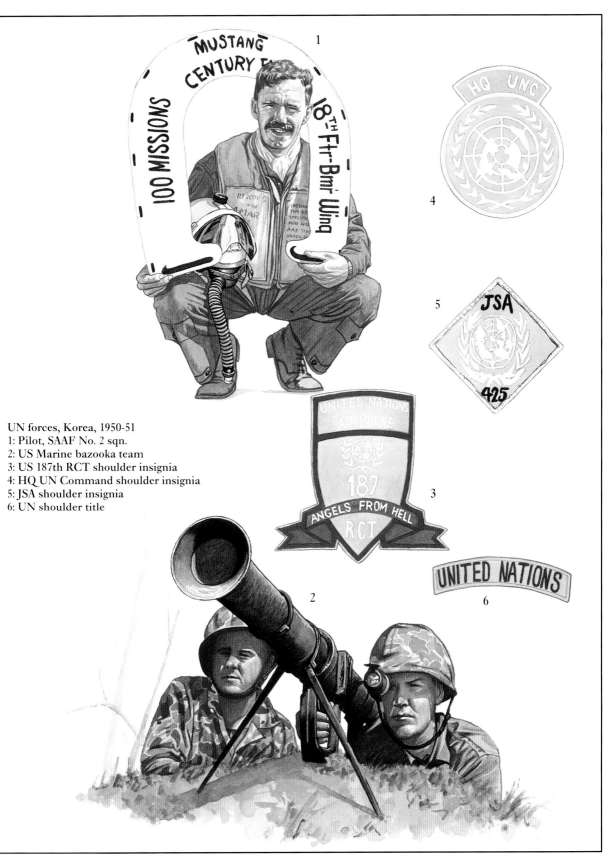

UN forces, Korea, 1950-51
1: Pilot, SAAF No. 2 sqn.
2: US Marine bazooka team
3: US 187th RCT shoulder insignia
4: HQ UN Command shoulder insignia
5: JSA shoulder insignia
6: UN shoulder title

A

1: Austrian Zugsführer, UNTSO, 1990
2: Swedish infantryman, UNTSO, 1980

3: Polish ensign, UNEF (II), 1979
4: UNTSO Medic's badge
5: UNEF Canadian Contingent badge

B

1: British infantryman, UNFICYP, 1992
2: Iranian infantryman, UNDOF, 1979
3: Finnish Contingent, UNDOF, 1990
4: Silver officer's badge
5: Aviation officer's bullion badge

C

1: Fijian infantryman, UNIFIL, 1991
2: Ghanaian infantryman, UNIFIL, 1990
3: Norwegian infantryman, UNIFIL, 1990
4: UNIFIL Signals badge
5: UN Field Service badge

D

1: Sgt., Australian Engineers,
   UNTAG, 1989
2: Sgt., Singaporean infantry,
   UNIKOM, 1992
3: Venezuelan infantryman,
   ONUSAL, 1992
4: General issue beret badge
5: Officer's bullion badge

E

1

2

3

4

United Nations pocket badges; see text commentary for detailed caption

5

6

7

8

9

10

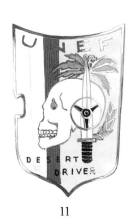

11

12

F

G

Nordic Training Centre, Finland
1: NTC emblem
2: Medical training
3: MP dog training
4: Finnish national emblem

H

Gulf War, 1991
1: Syrian sergeant
2: French Marine infantryman
3: Saudi Arabian private
4: Kuwaiti lieutenant-general

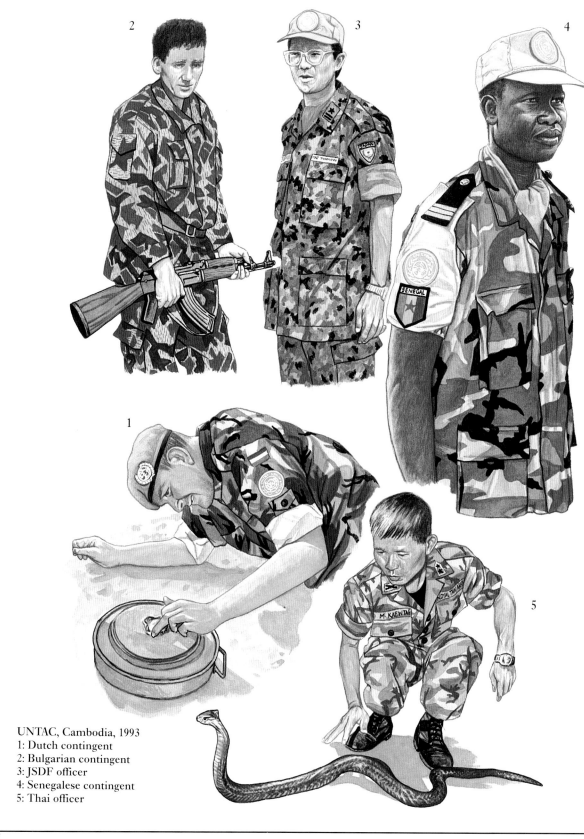

UNTAC, Cambodia, 1993
1: Dutch contingent
2: Bulgarian contingent
3: JSDF officer
4: Senegalese contingent
5: Thai officer

J

UNOSOM, Somalia, 1993
1: Italian paratrooper
2: UAE corporal
3: Pakistani infantryman
4: Belgian paratrooper
5: German
   Oberfeldwebel

K

UNPROFOR,
former Yugoslavia, 1993
1: Ukrainian Bn., Sarajevo
2: Spanish contingent, Bosnia
3: British infantryman, Vitez
4: French Officer, Zagreb
5: US infantryman, Macedonia

L

Australian UNOSOM troops in Baidoa, April 93. Both wear the Australian spot-pattern camouflage uniform with 'digger' hats; no UN insignia are visible. (United Nations/M.

PEACE-KEEPING IN THE 1990s

and ultimately the decision by President Clinton to withdraw US forces from Somalia by March 1994.

UNOSOM had been seen as a paradigm for the post-Cold War role of the United Nations – the first peace-keeping mission mandated under Chapter 7 of the UN charter (allowing the use of offensive force to achieve the objectives of UN resolutions) since the end of the Cold War, and an important test case for future missions. Though the outcome, and its effect on the reputation of the UN, remains unclear at the time of writing, what is clear is that the United States and 26 other countries successfully, if briefly, assisted a nation in chaos – the first time that the UN has militarily intervened in support of humanitarian aid – but violated international borders and national sovereignty in doing

The United Nations Charter has a stated goal of peace, justice and respect for human rights. Due to the frustration of the Cold War, subsequent conflicting spheres of influence, and lack of co-operation among the major powers to end regional conflicts, the UN charter remained unfulfilled. With the end of the Cold War and the reluctance of the only post-Cold War superpower – the United States under the Clinton Administration – to assume the role, the UN has now begun to 'wage peace' in earnest, assuming a position as the world's policeman. In 1993 the UN spent an estimated $3.8 billion on peace-keeping activities – five times what was spent in 1991 – with more than 600,000 troops deployed under UN auspices worldwide. Requests for another 14 peace-keeping missions are under consideration at the time of writing.

The Security Council is now seen as an international

organization using coercion and force for universal good. The UN, still learning how to operate in a post–Cold War environment, has continued to make mistakes. Though there have been some bright spots in the history of peace-keeping (the UN mission to Namibia/UNTAG and the mission to El Salvador/ONUSAL are good examples), other missions have been fraught with mistakes and miscalculations that have cost the lives of numerous peace-keepers and civilians.

In Somalia (UNOSOM) the troops were ill-prepared for their mission, with an inadequate mandate, and an inadequate understanding of a complicated situation on the ground – where power-hungry heavily armed factions roamed at will. These shortcomings were compounded by a lack of UN financial resources and personnel. These factors led to the deaths of 23 Pakistani peace-keepers on 5 June 1993, ambushed in their thin-skinned vehicles they ran out of ammunition before help could arrive and were massacred. The US quick-reaction

force sent to rescue the peace-keepers were sent to the wrong location twice, and finally found the Pakistanis by following the sound of gunfire. Earlier, the Pakistani contingent commander was forced to order food for his unit using his personal credit card.

In Cambodia, where UNTAC is regarded as a model peace-keeping operation – having cost $3 billion and involved the virtual rebuilding and running of the country – there is still a danger of the collapse of democracy due to the intransigence of the Khmer Rouge faction. The first Bulgarian peace-keeper unit sent to UNTAC was reportedly recruited directly from Bulgarian prisons, with the result that numerous infractions occurred before the unit was quickly withdrawn. Philippine peace-keepers were caught smuggling AK-47 rifles back to the Philippines. For the first time since the Second World War Japan committed forces outside its borders, but the killing of two Japanese peace-keepers and the subsequent public outcry puts future Japanese participation in doubt.

In Bosnia (UNPROFOR) local militias have looted aid convoys, one individual has turned back an entire column of relief supplies, while UN drivers have been indiscriminately killed. Some of the peace-keepers themselves have been accused of black market activities

Turkish UNOSOM troops providing area security; Mogadishu, April 1993. All wear the Turkish version of the woodland-type camouflage uniform and armour vest and carry G3 rifles; the Turkish national emblem is worn on the left shoulder. (United Nations/M. Grant)

nging from trading cigarettes and prostitution to
ling protection and drug-smuggling. The UN's mis-
n management is poor, as evidenced by the fact that
nadian General Lewis MacKenzie was given just three
ys to complete the planning for the establishment,
ployment, and logistics for the entire force. He
timates that he spent half that time struggling with the
N bureaucracy. The Jordanian contingent arrived in
mmer clothing during the winter months, while two
-prepared Nigerian soldiers froze to death. In the
urdish areas of northern Iraq UNIKOM was forced to
thdraw 50 peace-keepers in May 1993 due to funding
oblems.

Though problems and horror stories abound, the
N has also learned valuable lessons for the future,
cluding the power of public opinion, the need for
ilitary superiority, and the need for law and order. The
eration in Somalia (UNOSOM) was prompted by the
rce of public opinion; the media generated an
otional response when, in the US alone during 1992,
ey broadcast 468 news reports on the suffering in
malia, but only six reports on the suffering in
ighbouring Sudan, a country with a far worse plight.

The UN has learned that public opinion and
otionalism must not provoke a hurried action without
oper planning and co-ordination. The absolute neces-
y of a strong co-ordinated military organization was
own in Somalia. The first UN unit of 500 Pakistani
ace-keepers were kept virtual prisoners in their
mpound by marauding war lords who out-manned and
t-gunned the UN forces. It was not until the US and
her nations arrived in force for Operation 'Restore
pe' that a sense of relative calm returned to the area
hich lasted until the UN made the error of taking sides
the conflict and attempted to arrest General Aidid).
e UN has learned that law and order must be upheld,
ating a stable situation in which peace-keeping may
nction.

Changes are being made at the UN. To resolve some
the communication problems a 'situation room' has
en established in New York, this is staffed 24 hours a
y and equipped with modern telephones and fax
chines – replacing the '9 to 5' operation of a year ago,
ich relied on standard long-distance telephone lines
communication. The UN still lacks financial support
its operations. In 1993 unpaid member nation peace-
eping bills totalled over $1.5 billion.

Much has been written in the press regarding the
ure of UN operations. It is generally agreed that the
es for peace-keeping in the 1990s must include:
cognizable and attainable goals; actions conducted in
ncert with nations contributing peace-keepers; com-

mand and control of forces by contributing nations;
establishment of a UN Peace-keeping Command with a
command and control, administrative, and logistical
structure similar to that used by the Coalition Forces in
the Gulf War; predesignation and training of these forces
specifically for peace-keeping; establishment of a doctrine
for peace-keeping; further definition of the rules of
engagement; and the periodic training of different
national peace-keeping forces in combined operations.

Good intentions and expanding commitments aside,
the UN still lacks the organization, logistics, training,
financial resources, and commitment to police the many
struggles and civil wars taking place around the world.
However the UN remains the only world organization
involved in peace-making, peace-enforcement, and
peace-building. With continued member support, re-
organization and the benefit of experience there can still
be hope that the United Nations will make progress
towards guaranteeing world peace, justice and respect for
human rights.

THE PLATES

A: The Korean War
A1: Union of South Africa Air Force pilot, 1951
By 29 June 1950 most British Commonwealth forces
were pledged to the UN for action in Korea. The South
Africans' long-standing opposition to military action
with other Commonwealth forces, the belief that Korea
was not in their sphere of interest, and the long time
needed for mobilization caused vacillation over a troop
commitment. On 4 August 1950 the decision was
reached to send a contingent to Korea consisting of
South African Air Force Liaison HQ based in Tokyo,
and 2 Squadron SAAF; the South African government
ensured that the unit be attached, for political and
military reasons, to the US Air Force. On 25 September
49 officers and 157 other ranks of 2 Squadron arrived in
Yokohama and commenced operational training with F-
51D Mustang fighters and other equipment purchased
from the US. On 16 November five aircraft and
supporting personnel were flown to airfield K-9 near
Pusan, with the mission of ground attack and interdic-
tion, from where their first combat sortie was flown.
Attached to the US 18th Fighter-Bomber Wing, the unit
moved to airfield K-24 near Pyongyang, North Korea;
evacuated to airfield K-13 near Suwon; then moved to a
permanent base in South Korea at airfield K-10 near
Chinhae on 17 December 1950. Other elements of the
squadron moved from Japan to K-10, where the entire
unit operated for two years until re-equipped with US

F-86F Sabre jets in January 1953. The South Africans destroyed a total of 44 armoured vehicles, 891 other vehicles, over 400 supply points, and 1,000 buildings during the war. Both the US and Republic of Korea Presidential Unit Citations for gallantry were awarded to the unit. Here a South African pilot celebrating his 100th mission wears issue US flight gear including hard flight helmet with Type A-14 demand oxygen mask, AN-S-31A summer flying suit, B-5 pneumatic life vest, and 'rough-out' leather service shoes. The flight helmet was the only 'modern' piece of equipment issued: the oxygen mask was standardized in 1943 and the flight suit and life vest in 1944.

A2: US Marine 3.5-inch rocket launcher team, summer 1950
Both figures wear the World War Two M1 helmet with reversible spot-pattern camouflage covers. The gunner on the right wears the Model 1944 pattern green HBT utility uniform while the loader wears the Model 1944 reversible camouflage HBT utilities. All web gear and packs have been stowed in their emplacement. The M20 3.5in. rocket launcher, or 'super bazooka', replaced the smaller 2.36in. weapon of World War Two fame. The M20 fires an 8.61lb. (3.9kg) rocket that can penetrate 11 inches (28cm) of homogeneous armour plate.

A3: UN Airborne, US 187th Regimental Combat Team, shoulder sleeve insignia

A4: Headquarters UN Command shoulder sleeve insignia

A5: Joint Security Area shoulder sleeve insignia

A6: United Nations tab

B1: Austrian Zugsführer, UNTSO, 1990
The United Nations Truce Supervision Organization for Palestine dates from May 1948. The Austrian contingent has served with UNTSO from 1967 to the present. Here a Zugsführer wears the green fatigue uniform with UN bilingual shoulder sleeve insignia and UN blue beret with metal badge. The Steyr AUG 5.56mm rifle is carried.

B2: Swedish infantryman, UNTSO, 1980
The Swedish military has maintained contingents to UNTSO from 1948 to the present; five UNTSO Chiefs of Staff have been Swedish Army generals. Here a member of the Swedish Infantry Battalion attached to UNTSO wears green fatigue uniform, a blue cap with

UN insignia, and carries a blue-painted helmet with both 'UN' and global projection insignia. Tan brassards on both shoulders display the Swedish national emblem and UN shoulder sleeve insignia. The weapon is the 9mm Carl Gustaf Model 45 sub-machine gun.

B3: Polish ensign, UNEF(II), 1979
Polish troops were deployed as part of UNDOF, UNGOMAP, UNIIMOG, UNTAG, UNIKOM, MINURSO, UNPROFOR, and UNTAC. For UNEF (II) Poland provided logistics, engineering, medical and transport units from late 1973 to early 1980; and instituted a mine-clearing course in early 1974. Here a Polish engineer ensign (Chorazy) wears the grey 'worm' pattern camouflage uniform first seen in the late 1960 with rubberized rank insignia, and a tan brassard with white on red Polish eagle and 'POLSKA'. More often seen wearing a 'worm'-camouflage rogatywka field ca this Pole wears the UN blue cap.

B4: UNTSO medical services metal beret badge

B5: UNEF Canada Contingent metal beret badge

C1: British infantryman, UNFICYP, 1992
The United Nations Peacekeeping Force in Cyprus was established in March 1964. The United Kingdom has maintained a presence in Cyprus since that date including infantry, force reserves, air units, and medical personnel. The British contingent (BRITCON) is the largest in the Force and was stationed island-wide prior to 1974; they were then redeployed west of the Nicosia International Airport in the Buffer Zone, Sector Two. The British Brigadier A.J. Wilson was the Force Commander from December 1965 to May 1966. This figure wears the two-colour desert camouflage uniform introduced for the Gulf War, UN blue beret with metal insignia, issue blue ascot, and the British national emblem on his left sleeve under the UN white on blue shoulder sleeve insignia. He carries the SA80 5.56mm rifle with a Susat 4× optical sight.

C2: Iranian infantryman, UNDOF, 1979
One year after the 1973 Arab-Israeli War the United Nations Disengagement Force was established to monitor the separation of Syrian and Israeli troops along the Golan Heights. The Shah of Iran, Western-leaning and seeking influence not only in the Gulf but also as a world player, deployed infantry as part of UNDOF in August 1975. The UNDOF contingent was disbanded in March 1979 following the Iranian revolution. Here the seldom seen two-colour green 'splotch' uniform, cut like a U

gle jacket, is worn without UN insignia; the German 3 7.62mm rifle is carried.

3: Finnish Contingent, UNDOF, 1990
nland has contributed over 30,000 military personnel UN peace-keeping operations since 1956, and infantry its to UNDOF since March 1979, with participation heduled to cease at the end of 1993. Two UNDOF mmanders have been Finnish generals: Erkki Kaira om February 1981 to May 1982 and Gustav Hagglund om June 1985 to May 1986. This soldier wears green igues with climbing boots, UN blue cap with bilingual signia, a blue field-expedient vest, and a tan brassard the left shoulder displaying the Finnish Army/ tional emblem and UN shoulder sleeve insignia. He rries the Finnish 7.62×39mm M62 assault rifle with e standard infantry tubular folding stock.

4: Silver bullion officer's beret badge

group of Finnish
ldiers undergoing
eckpoint training at the
nited Nations Nordic
raining Centre,
inisalo, Finland. First
tablished in 1969, the

Centre provides training
for UN military observers
from Finland, Denmark,
Norway, Sweden and
Switzerland. (Finnish
Ministry of Defense)

C5: UN aviation brigade officer's gold bullion beret badge on white wool

D1: UNIFIL, Fijian private, 1991
The United Nations Interim Force in Lebanon was established in March 1978, and since May 1978 Fiji has deployed one infantry battalion of 726 soldiers to UNIFIL; they have taken numerous casualties. Fiji's commitment to UNIFIL is impressive considering that the all-volunteer Fijian Army has only 4,700 personnel (organized into one engineer squadron, one artillery troop, and four infantry battalions). Other deployments include UNGOMAP, UNTAG, UNIKOM, and UNTAC. This private wears green fatigues with national emblem and private's stripe on the right shoulder, UN blue beret with metal insignia, and blue PASGT armour vest. UN shoulder sleeve insignia is worn on the left arm, obscured here.

D2: Ghanaian infantryman, UNIFIL, 1990
Ghana has contributed one infantry battalion and an integrated headquarters command, consisting of a defence platoon and an engineer platoon, from September 1979 to the present. A force Mobile Reserve consisting of a composite mechanized company organized in January

An early UN issue brassard: blue wool, 9×17cm, with a direct-embroidered white thread 8cm diameter bi-lingual UN insignia in the centre (Author's photo)

1987 included Ghanaian troops. Ghana has contributed to 11 UN missions/forces. Here the German-manufactured metal helmet, a DPM camouflage armour vest, woodland camouflage pattern fatigues and issue boots are worn; the rifle is the German G3.

D3: Norwegian infantryman, UNIFIL, 1990

The Norwegians have been participants in UNIFIL since March 1978, providing infantry, logistics, medical, and maintenance personnel. This Norwegian soldier is engaged in a form of preventive diplomacy – he is befriending a local Lebanese child. The soldier wears green fatigues with UN shoulder sleeve insignia, a faded UN blue beret with metal insignia, and a US-manufactured PASGT woodland camouflage armour vest. He carries the Norwegian-made version of the German G3, adopted in 1964.

D4: UNIFIL Signals metal beret badge.

D5: UN Field Service metal beret badge

E1: Australian sergeant, UNTAG, 1989

The United Nations Assistance Group in Namibia was a bright spot in UN peace-keeping, representing a model of co-operation among the 50 nations involved with the successful completion of the mission. This Australian military engineer wears the UN blue beret with metal insignia, the Australian spot-pattern camouflage uniform, and a camouflage brassard bearing both UN shoulder sleeve insignia and the Australian national emblem of a yellow kangaroo on a dark green field with white lettering. Rank insignia, worn on the right shoulder, are

not visible. Other national insignia for UN du consisted of a yellow disc with a black kangar superimposed on a green map of Australia, with r lettering ('AUSTRALIA') and a red border, worn eith on camouflage or green brassards.

E2: Singaporean sergeant, UNIKOM, 1992

The United Nations Iraq-Kuwait Observation Missi was established in April 1991. Thirty-five nations ha contingents deployed as part of UNIKOM, including t Republic of Singapore, a relatively small country whi nevertheless spends 5.5 per cent of its gross natio product on defence. Singapore has contributed troops UNTAG in Namibia, UNIKOM, and UNTAC Cambodia. This sergeant wears the Singaporean woo land pattern camouflage uniform, UN blue beret w cloth badge, and UN blue armour vest.

E3: Venezuelan infantryman, ONUSAL, 1992

The United Nations Observer Mission in El Salvad was established in July 1991. This Venezuelan milita observer wears the UN issue blue cap with biling insignia, Venezuelan issue woodland pattern fatigu with national emblem on the left shoulder, green w gear, and carries the FN FAL rifle.

E4: UN general issue metal beret badge

E5: Gold bullion officer's beret badge on white wool

F: United Nations pocket badges

The longer the duration of the peace-keeping force

server mission, and the greater the number of nations volved, the more numerous and varied the badges and her unit insignia. Local manufacture has added to the riations. The following is a selection of pocket badges ed by various contingents. *F1:* UNTSO Observer roup Egypt. *F2:* Dutch Bn., UNIFIL. *F3:* HQ NDOF. *F4:* FIN BATT Guard of Honour (Finnish n.). *F5:* Austrian Aviation, Rotary Wing. *F6:* Polish ontingent UNEF. *F7:* AUSBATT-1, UNEF II, NEF (Austrian Bn.). *F8:* GHANBATT – 3rd (Ghana neral use badge). *F9:* SWEDCON, UNEF II (Swedish n.). *F10:* Military Police Middle East (general use dge). *F11:* UNEF desert driver (UNEF I). *F12:* UN igineers – on leather fob.

: United Nations Service Medals

he United Nations has issued three versions of the rvice medal; Korea Service (1950 to 1953), UNEF ervice (1956 to 1967), and a standard medal for all later issions distinguished by specific ribbons.

The **Korean Service Medal (G1 and G2)** was tablished by General Assembly Resolution 483(V) and opted on 12 December 1950. The medal was issued on September 1951, to be awarded to all members of ilitary forces (and armed forces of the Republic of orea) who served on behalf of the United Nations in orea. The period of eligibility was 30 days except for itish and Commonwealth forces, which was one day xcept for periods of inspection which had to total 30 ys). The medal was struck in the Amhirio (Ethiopian), utch, English, French, Greek, Italian, Korean, Span- , Thai, Turkish, Tagalog (Philippine), and Flemish nguages. The largest number of medals struck was the nglish version (2,761,732) with the smallest number for lian non-combatants (130). The bronze alloy medal is mm in diameter with a 35mm wide ribbon of nine UN ue and eight white stripes. The obverse of the medal picts the UN emblem of a polar projection map of the

world encircled by two olive branches of peace. The reverse of the medal has the inscription 'For service in defence of the principles of the charter of the United Nations'. The bar, an integral part of the claw and straight iron suspension, reads 'KOREA'. It was anticipated that different bars would be issued for later UN actions.

Following the Arab-Israeli War the United Nations Emergency Force (UNEF) was established to patrol the Israeli-Egyptian border. A medal for **UNEF Service (G3 and G4)** was authorized in accordance with Resolution 1001(S) on 7 November 1956. The obverse was patterned after the Korea Service Medal with the addition of 'UNEF' and the inscription 'In the service of peace' on the reverse. The bronze alloy medal is 35mm in diameter with a 37mm wide ribbon. Any personnel serving with UNEF for a period of 90 days were authorized the medal. Only one coinage was struck, with 47,037 medals awarded (the maximum strength of UNEF at any one time was 6,073 personnel).

The **UN Medal (G5 and G6)** was developed in July 1959 as a general award to personnel serving with the United Nations as observers or otherwise maintaining order. The ribbon colours and arrangement signify specific mission/forces. The medal is almost identical to the UNEF medal, but with 'UN' replacing 'UNEF'.

G1: Korean Service Medal English Version (Obverse). *G2:* Korean Service Medal – English version (Reverse). *G3:* UNEF Service Medal (Obverse). *G4:* UNEF Service Medal (Reverse). *G5:* UN Standard

Locally manufactured insignia, with white letters and outlines on a blue background, for Russian peace-keepers. The UN global projection is worn on the right shoulder, the Russian tricolour national emblem on the left, the 'Russia' tab over the right breast pocket, and the blood group over the left. The insignia also exists in a subdued black-on-green version. (Author's photo)

Medal (Obverse) (Ribbon for UNIKOM Service). **G6:** UN Standard Medal (Reverse) (Ribbon for UNIKOM Service. **G7:** Ribbons for UN Standard Medal: *(a)* UNTSO/UNOGIL; *(b)* UNTEA; *(c)* UNFICYP; *(d)* UNDOF; *(e)* UNMOGIP/UNIPOM; *(f)* UNOC; *(g)* UNEF II; *(h)* UNYOM; *(i)* UNIFIL; *(j)* UNIIMOG; *(k)* UNAVEM; *(l)* UNTAG; *(m)* ONUCA; *(n)* MINURSO; *(o)* ONUSAL; *(p)* UNAMIC; *(q)* UNPROFOR; *(r)* UNTAC; *(s)* UN General Service (New York headquarters).

H: UN Nordic Training Centre, Niinisalo, Finland, 1992

The long history of Finnish commitment to UN service resulted in the establishment in 1969 of the UN Training Centre, attached to the Satakunta Artillery Regiment at Niinisalo, with a training contingent of two officers. In 1982 the name was changed to the UN Nordic Training Centre. The current training staff consists of 35 personnel, with the responsibility for selecting and calling up personnel from the reserve in order to complete training for UN service; installing personnel in their units; equipping the unit while ensuring logistics and supply, and arranging transport. In addition the Centre provides training for UN military observers, military police personnel, staff officers, and logistics and transport personnel from Denmark, Norway, Sweden, and Switzerland. The largest training group – military observers – take instructions in three organized courses, producing 150 graduates annually.

H1: Nordic Training Centre emblem

H2: Medical training
Here a Swedish medic (left) assists in bandaging the leg of a Finnish soldier (foreground). The Swede wears the issue Model 1990 camouflage uniform, wool cap, and boots. A Swiss officer (right) takes the lead in the simulated first aid; he wears the Model 73 one-piece camouflage overall for armour troops, issue hiking boots, and grey cap.

H3: Dog-handling training
Here two Finnish Army military police personnel conduct exercises with a German Shepherd police dog. The man on the left wears one colour variant of the Finnish camouflage uniform, boots, and headgear; at right is a padded dog-handling suit.

H4: Finnish Army national emblem

I: The Gulf War, 1991

I1: Syrian sergeant
President Assad of Syria, desiring an end to his country isolation as a terrorist, anti-American state, dispatched advance party of 1,000 troops to Saudi Arabia in Augu 1990. The contingent eventually totalled 19,000 a consisted of a special forces regiment and the 9 Armoured Division equipped with 200 T-55 and T- tanks; an additional unit of 500–600 paratroopers w stationed in the United Arab Emirates. The Syria though reporting to Joint Forces Command North, we regarded with suspicion and were not fully trusted wi intelligence information. They fought a small engag ment with the Iraqis on 5 February, but were placed Corps reserve in support of the Saudi, Kuwaiti, a Egyptian units who led the attack on 24 February 199 This soldier wears the Soviet L-1 chemical protecti suit with ShMS mask and rubber gloves to comple the outfit. The Soviet AKM 7.62×39mm rifle carried.

I2: French Marine Infantryman
French involvement in what was to become the G War started in September 1990 when units of the *For d'Action Rapide* were deployed to Saudi Arabia, oste sibly to counter the Iraqi violation of the Kuwait C French Embassy and the abduction of three consul officials. By January 1991 13,300 French milita personnel were deployed to Saudi Arabia as part of th Operation 'Daguet' ('Dagger'). President Mitterra attempted to find a diplomatic solution to the crisis a kept military activities on a low level, avoiding joi exercises with US and other forces; the Fren committed themselves to the defence of Saudi Arab only, avoiding participation in offensive actions. Fren public opinion changed the decision, however, and t French decided to take an active role in the liberation Kuwait. The French contingent in the Gulf War serv with distinction, and their skill was emphasized in t successful performance of a deep-thrust armour offensive which contributed to the Iraqi defeat. T Marine, or Corporal Chef, is shown participating in ceremony in Kuwait City after the war. He wears t four-pocket desert camouflage uniform with para embellishments including a yellow lanyard and *epaulet de tradition*, national insignia on the left shoulder, ran and unit badges. His *kepi* and bugle banner both displ the Marine troops emblem.

I3: Saudi Arabian private
With oil dollars providing state-of-the-art Weste equipment, training, and infrastructure, the Kingdom Saudi Arabia assumed leadership of the Arab sta

posed to Iraq and requested Western intervention to
unter the invasion of Kuwait. Saudi Arabia played a
ajor role in the war by providing logistics and other
rvices, fuel, water, and excellent base facilities to the
ti-Iraqi forces. The Saudi armed forces consist of the
,000-man Saudi Arabian Land Force, and a 56,000-
an National Guard. Other organizations include the
r Force, Navy, Air-Defence, Frontier Force, Coast
uard, and a Saudi Peninsular Shield Force composed
units from all Gulf Co-operation Council states. This
udi private, or *Jundi*, wears the US M1 helmet with
60s-vintage reversible helmet cover with brown side
owing; Korean-made six-colour daytime desert BDU;

US-made ALICE gear and desert boots in tan colour,
and a US M17A1 gas mask in a green carrier. He carries
a version of the HK/G3 7.62 NATO rifle with metal
telescoping stock.

I4: Kuwaiti lieutenant-general

Prior to the Gulf War the Kuwaiti Army consisted of
16,000 troops in two armoured, one mechanized, and one
artillery brigade led by a professional British-trained
officer corps. Unable to withstand the multi-divisional
Iraqi attack spearheaded by the Republican Guard, 4,500
Kuwaiti personnel escaped to Saudi Arabia with their
equipment. Army personnel who were not killed or taken

vo UNYOM Yugoslav
diers on patrol near
jran, Saudi Arabia, July
53. (United Nations)

prisoner remained in Kuwait to form the underground resistance movement. The Kuwaiti Army in exile was rebuilt with the 4,500 troops at the core; an additional 10,500 Kuwaiti citizens returned from other countries or infiltrated through Iraqi lines. Military training was provided in Saudi Arabia, the United Arab Emirates and the United States. Numerous brigades were formed, and participated in rear area security, mine clearance and urban combat, and the liberation of Kuwait City. It was estimated that as many as 4,200 Kuwaitis were killed and 12,000 taken prisoner. Here a Kuwaiti lieutenant-general, or *Fariq*, cuts a ribbon during a ceremony following the end of the Gulf War. He wears a black beret with gold bullion insignia, a variation of the three-colour brown DPM camouflage uniform seen so often in use in the Gulf, and gold bullion-on-tan shoulder rank slip-ons of a crown over crossed swords.

J: United Nations Transitional Authority in Cambodia, 1993

J1: Royal Netherlands Army private, UN Mine Clearance Unit

Here a Netherlands private instructs Cambodians in procedures for removing one of the millions of mines that were scattered throughout the country during th war. He wears the UN blue beret with metal badg Dutch-issue three-pocket DPM shirt with nation emblem and UN bilingual shoulder sleeve insignia on th left shoulder, and khaki shorts. Often seen in use b Dutch members of the mine clearance unit were local manufactured insignia with white letters on a blue fiel in both the Khmer and English languages, worn ov both breast pockets to identify the wearer's surname an unit. Other contingent members wore brassards wi identifying national emblems, country and/or unit tab and variants of the standard UN shoulder sleeve insigni

J2: Bulgarian private

As a result of the end of the Cold War and the break-u of the Warsaw Pact the Bulgarians deployed a small un to Cambodia – their first UN mission – along wi troops from their former Warsaw Pact allies Hungar Poland and Russia. This soldier wears the Bulgarian tw piece 'splinter' pattern camouflage uniform devoid insignia, and carries the Polish-manufactured AKS rifl

Examples of national insignia usually worn on either a green or tan brassard. Each woven insignia measures 5×8cm (Author's photo)

Examples of US camouflage brassards: that on the left an Army 10th Mountain Division Military Police brassard for Baidoa and Mogadishu, Somalia (UNOSOM), that on the right an Air Force Security Police brassard for Riyadh, Saudi Arabia (Gulf War). (Author's collection)

: Japanese Self Defense Force major

ter years of 'chequebook diplomacy', under pressure om the United States and other nations, and amid uch controversy at home, Japan committed troops tside her borders for the first time since World War wo, sending a force to Cambodia under UN command. panese television broadcasts glamorized the role of the N peace-keeper, with the result that enlistment in the DF rose 27% over the previous year. After reviewing nsportation problems in resupply operations in Cam- dia (and in the hope of permanent membership on the N Security Council), the Japanese Defense Agency oposed the purchase of US-manufactured C-17 long- nge heavy transport aircraft in the 1996–2000 time me as a display of commitment to participation in ture UN-sponsored humanitarian and peace-keeping ssions. (The exaggerated public response to minimal DF casualties in Cambodia casts some doubt on future mmitments, however.) Here a JSDF engineer major ars the 'flektar' camouflage uniform with full colour tional emblem on the left shoulder, UN bilingual oulder sleeve insignia on the right (obscured here), ite-lettered 'JAPAN' on blue tape over the right east pocket, and blue visored cap with UN insignia.

J4: Senegalese Contingent

The troop commitment to UNTAC was the fourth UN operation in which the Senegalese participated, previous missions being UNIFIL, UNIIMOG, and UNIKOM. Here the blue cap with UN bilingual insignia is worn, with a lightweight woodland camouflage BDU jacket, and a tan brassard on the right shoulder displaying the national insignia and UN shoulder sleeve insignia.

J5: Royal Thai Army lieutenant

The Thais have been involved in the many Indo-Chinese conflicts due to proximity and alliances, so it was no surprise that a Royal Thai Army contingent would serve with UNTAC. This officer wears one of the many copies of US ERDL and woodland camouflage uniforms seen in use by Thai forces, with all insignia embroidered on matching camouflage material, and no UN insignia worn. His boots are a copy of US jungle boots.

K: United Nations Operation in Somalia (UNOSOM), 1993

K1: Italian paratrooper

At the time of writing the Italian commitment to UNOSOM, code-named Operation 'Ibis', consists of approximately 2,000 infantry, 290 Marines, and some 80 airmen. The 186th and 187th Airborne Regiments, the 9th Airborne Battalion 'Col. Moshin', the 'San Marco' Marine Battalion, and the combat divers of CONSUBIN have contributed troops. They are supported by ten M60 MBTs from the Ariete Armoured Division, four Centauro recce vehicles, 23 assorted helicopters, 31 GG 14 armoured vehicles, and an Air Force contingent of two G-222s and two helicopters. This paratrooper wears the Italian desert camouflage uniform developed as a result of the Gulf War, and the Israeli Ephod load-bearing equipment. He carries the BM-59 7.62mm rifle with folding stock.

K2: United Arab Emirates corporal

The United Arab Emirates deployed 690 troops to UNOSOM, their first international commitment since participation in the Gulf War. This corporal, or 'Arif, wears the British-made GS Mk 6 combat helmet with a Korean-made six-colour daytime desert camouflage cover, Korean-made daytime desert BDU with national emblem and rank affixed, black leather gloves, and a point blank armour vest with a tan cover.

K3: Pakistani Contingent

A Pakistani contingent of 500 lightly armed troops was the first UN unit to be deployed to Somalia. Out-gunned and out-numbered, they were virtual prisoners in their compound until US Marine and other personnel landed during Operation 'Restore Hope'. This perceived weakness may have been a factor in the ambush on 5 June 1993 of a Pakistani patrol, which left 24 peace-keepers dead. The consequent passing of UN Security Council Resolution 837, calling for the punishment of those responsible, led to an inexorable escalation in violence; to increasing military and civilian casualties; and finally to the announced withdrawal of the US contingent.

This Pakistani soldier carries a Soviet-bloc RPG; he wears a faded UN blue beret with metal insignia, tan shirt and trousers with full-colour insignia, UN blue ascot, and national insignia hand-embroidered on green wool. Pakistanis could be seen on patrol in Mogadishu wearing this uniform with the addition of sky blue-painted US M1 helmets and US PASGT armour vests in woodland camouflage. In mid-1993 the Pakistanis could be seen wearing woodland and desert woodland type camouflage uniforms with tan brassards for display of the Pakistani national emblem and UN shoulder sleeve insignia, with PASGT woodland camouflage armour vests and helmets. Their weapons remain the Soviet RPG, AK-47/AKM family, and German G3/HK rifles.

K4: Belgian Army sergeant

On 13 December 1992 a detachment of Belgian paratroops from 11 Co., 1 Para Battalion were flown directly from their home base at Diest in eight C-130 Hercules aircraft, landing in Mogadishu after a stop in Addis Ababa. With the mission to secure the harbour and airport, the Belgian parats landed with a detachment of 250 US Marines on a small beach in Kismayo at dawn on 20 December; after the area was secure the remainder of the unit landed at Kismayo airport. Deployed for months, the Belgian contingent would eventually total 900 troops, operating under US command to ensure control of Kismayo. This sergeant wears the issue green T-shirt, webbing, and red beret with a Para badge, British lightweight body armour with two-colour desert DPM cover, and Belgian-pattern 1958 or 'jigsaw' camouflage trousers. He carries the Belgian FN 5.56mm rifle.

K5: German Oberfeldwebel

Amid much controversy, the first overseas deployment of German troops since World War Two was ordered with the mission to provide humanitarian aid to Somalia. Critics argued that Chancellor Helmut Kohl's decision to send a total of 1,700 soldiers to Somalia was an attempt to improve Germany's image abroad, and that participation in UNOSOM was too dangerous for German troops with their strictly humanitarian mission. Mr. Kohl countered that Germany was accepting new international responsibilities and must expect that German soldiers would, while on UN-related missions, 'if necessary, put their lives on the line'. The first group of 50 German peace-keepers arrived in Mogadishu in preparation for moving to their area of operations in Belet Huen. This Oberfeldwebel wears the German-made UN blue beret with cloth insignia, the 'flektar' camouflage uniform, and an olive green brassard on the left shoulder bearing the national emblem, a subdued black-on-green 'German' tab, and bilingual UN shoulder sleeve insignia.

L: UNPROFOR; Croatia, Bosnia-Herzegovina and Macedonia, 1993

L1: Ukrainian Battalion, Sarajevo, Bosnia

In most Eastern-bloc armies it is considered that black

arket activities and foraging for food to augment low
y and meagre rations are a fact of life. However the
N force headquarters in Zagreb, Croatia, took a dim
ew of this practice. In summer 1993 13 members of the
krainian battalion were sent home and dishonourably
scharged for black market activities that included drug-
nuggling. This soldier wears the Ukrainian 'splotch'
mouflage uniform, similar to that used by the Soviet
rmy late in the Afghanistan War and often referred to
the Soviet woodland uniform, with both UN and
krainian shoulder sleeve insignia added. The AK–47S
45mm rifle, blue-painted helmet, and green armour
st are of Soviet origin.

2: Spanish Contingent, Bosnia

his Spanish soldier wears the UN blue beret with cloth
signia, the Spanish woodland camouflage uniform with
ational insignia on each shoulder, issue webbing, and
rries the Spanish CETME L 5.56mm rifle. Some
panish armoured unit members could be seen wearing
e Spanish version of the 'Fritz' kevlar helmet with blue
oth covers bearing the letters 'UN' in white; woodland

camouflage armour vests; camouflage webbing; and green
brassards with the national emblem, 'ESPANA' tab, and
UN shoulder sleeve insignia.

L3: British infantryman, Bosnia

The deployment of British forces – whose core has been
a mechanized infantry battalion with Warrior infantry
fighting vehicles – to the former Republic of Yugoslavia,
code-named Operation 'Grapple', began in early October
1992 and continued until the end of November with
2,300 troops deployed to Split, Croatia. At that time the
Split headquarters consisted of HQ 11 Armoured
Brigade, 360 Supply Company RAOC, and Signals
Squadron. Other bases include Tomislavgrad (then
including force logistics, Royal Engineers, HQ 5 Ordnance Battalion, 17 Squadron RCT); Gornji Vakuf
(initially B Company, 1st Battalion, Cheshire Regiment,
and 7 Armoured Workshop Company, REME); and
Vitez (initially remainder of Cheshire Regiment, one
company of Royal Irish Regiment, recce squadron of
9th/12th Royal Lancers, and support units). Units have
been rotated home at six-month intervals. The Vitez

n 11 June 1963 the United
Jations Observation
Iission in Yemen
UNYOM) was mandated
 ensure the maintenance
f peace in the area. Two
JNYOM Canadian
nilitary observers
iscussing map references
ith Prince El Turki,
iovernor of Gizan, Saudi
rabia, June 1963. (United
Jations)

Members of the Papuan Volunteer Corps, created in 1958 and consisting of 439 all ranks, under the command of Netherlands Lt.Col. van Heuvan (UNSF), return to their barracks after completing a training mission near Manokwari, New Guinea, November 1962. The UNSF was mandated to maintain peace in the region as established by Indonesia and the Netherlands. The mission was established in October 1962, concluded in April 1963, and consisted of over 1,500 UN personnel. (United Nations)

Right: Pakistani troops disembarking for yet another UN Observer Mission: West New Guinea, October 1962. (United Nations)

ce is tasked with escorting and protecting UN aid
nvoys; the rules of engagement allow the troops to
urn fire only if they come under attack. Here the
itish squaddie wears the GS Mk 6 combat helmet and
htweight body armour, both with UN blue covers; the
ue DPM jacket and trousers; and commercially
rchased Arktis DPM chest webbing – so often seen in
e by troops in Northern Ireland and the Gulf War.
he British national emblem and UN shoulder sleeve
signia are either displayed on a green brassard (as here)
affixed directly to the uniform. The weapon is the
ndard infantry version of the SA80.

4: French captain, Zagreb, Croatia
he first French contingent to UNPROFOR was de-
oyed to Krajina, Croatia, in April 1992. At that time the
ench Battalion consisted of five combat companies,
vice units, and one company of engineers with a total of
6 personnel and 254 vehicles. On 17 July the unit
ffered the first combat fatalities when two officers on
trol were killed by a remotely detonated mine. Here the
tin 300 uniform is worn with French national insignia
on the right shoulder, the sky blue-painted Model 1978 F1
helmet, and an armour vest with a woodland-type camouflage cover. (The armour vest is one of three types seen in
use by the French forces, the others being in green, and a
'lizard' or 'brush-stroke' camouflage.)

L5: US Army private, Macedonia
For the first time, US armed forces were placed under
UN command and deployed to the former Yugoslav
Republic of Macedonia as a peace-keeping force with the
mission of reporting any military activity along the
borders of Macedonia, Serbia, and Kosovo. In support of
Operation 'Able Sentry' a USAF Tactical Airlift Control
Squadron was first deployed to Skopje on 3 July 1993.
On 6 July 300 members of the Berlin Brigade were
airlifted into Macedonia to train and operate alongside
UN Scandinavian forces of NORDBAT. This member
of the brigade wears woodland camouflage BDUs, blue-
painted PASGT 'Fritz' helmet with white 'UN' lettering, and standard issue All-purpose Lightweight Individual Carrying Equipment (ALICE) gear. He carries
the M249 Squad Automatic Weapon (SAW).

UNITED NATIONS PEACE-KEEPING FORCE AND OBSERVER MISSION COMPOSITION

FORCE	FORCE COMPOSITION
UNTSO	Argentina, Australia, Austria, Belgium, Canada, Chile, China, Denmark, Finland, France, Ireland, Italy, Netherlands, New Zealand, Norway, Russia, Sweden, Switzerland, United States
UNMOGIP	Australia, Belgium, Canada, Chile, Denmark, Ecuador, Finland, Italy, Mexico, New Zealand, Norway, Sweden, Uruguay, United States
UNEF I	Brazil, Canada, Columbia, Denmark, Finland, India, Indonesia, Norway, Sweden, Yugoslavia
UNOGIL	Afghanistan, Argentina, Burma, Canada, Ceylon, Chile, Denmark, Ecuador, Finland, India, Indonesia, Ireland, Italy, Nepal, Netherlands, New Zealand, Norway, Peru, Portugal, Thailand
ONUC	Argentina, Austria, Brazil, Burma, Canada, Ceylon, Denmark, Ethiopia, Ghana, Guinea, India, Indonesia, Iran, Ireland, Italy, Liberia, Malaya, Mali, Morocco, Netherlands, Nigeria, Norway, Pakistan, Philippines, Sierra Leone, Sudan, Sweden, Tunisia, United Arab Republic, Yugoslavia
UNTEA/SF	Brazil, Canada, Ceylon, India, Ireland, Nigeria, Pakistan, Sweden, United States
UNYOM	Australia, Canada, Ceylon, Denmark, Ghana, India, Italy, Netherlands, Norway, Pakistan, Yugoslavia
UNFICYP	Australia, Austria, Canada, Denmark, Finland, Ireland, New Zealand, Sweden, United Kingdom
DOMREP	Brazil, Canada, Ecuador, India
UNIPOM	Australia, Belgium, Brazil, Burma, Canada, Ceylon, Chile, Denmark, Ethiopia, Finland, Ireland, Italy, Nepal, Netherlands, Nigeria, Norway, Sweden, Venezuela
UNEF II	Australia, Austria, Canada, Finland, Ghana, Indonesia, Ireland, Nepal, Panama, Peru, Poland, Senegal, Sweden
UNDOF	Austria, Canada, Finland, Iran, Peru, Poland
UNIFIL	Canada, Fiji, Finland, France, Ghana, Iran, Ireland, Italy, Nepal, Netherlands, Nigeria, Norway, Senegal, Sweden
UNGOMAP	Austria, Canada, Denmark, Fiji, Finland, Ghana, Ireland, Nepal, Poland, Sweden
UNIIMOG	Argentina, Australia, Austria, Bangladesh, Canada, Denmark, Finland, Ghana, Hungary, India, Indonesia, Ireland, Italy, Kenya, Malaysia, New Zealand, Nigeria, Norway, Peru, Poland, Senegal, Sweden, Turkey, Uruguay, Yugoslavia, Zambia
UNTAG	Australia, Austria, Bangladesh, Barbados, Belgium, Canada, China, Congo, Costa Rica, Czechoslovakia, Denmark, Egypt, Fiji, Finland, France, Germany, Ghana, Greece, Guyana, Hungary, India, Indonesia, Ireland, Italy, Jamaica, Japan, Kenya, Malaysia, Netherlands, New Zealand, Nigeria, Norway, Pakistan, Panama, Peru, Poland, Portugal, Singapore, Spain, Sudan, Sweden, Switzerland, Thailand, Togo, Trinidad & Tobago, Tunisia, USSR, United Kingdom, Yugoslavia
ONUCA	Argentina, Brazil, Canada, Columbia, Ecuador, Germany, India, Ireland, Spain, Sweden, Venezuela
UNIKOM	Argentina, Austria, Bangladesh, Canada, Chile, China, Denmark, Fiji, Finland, France, Ghana, Greece, Hungary, India, Indonesia, Ireland, Italy, Kenya, Malaysia, Nigeria, Norway, Pakistan, Poland, Romania, Russia, Senegal, Singapore, Sweden, Switzerland, Thailand, Turkey, United Kingdom, United States, Uruguay, Venezuela
UNAVEM	Algeria, Argentina, Brazil, Congo, Czechoslovakia, India, Jordan, Norway, Spain, Yugoslavia
ONUSAL	Argentina, Austria, Brazil, Canada, Chile, Columbia, Ecuador, France, Guyana, India, Italy, Mexico, Norway, Spain, Sweden, Venezuela
MINURSO	Argentina, Austria, Bangladesh, Belgium, Canada, China, Egypt, France, Ghana, Greece, Guinea, Honduras, Ireland, Italy, Kenya, Malaysia, Nigeria, Pakistan, Poland, Russia, Switzerland, Tunisia, United Kingdom, United States, Venezuela
UNPROFOR	Argentina, Austria, Bangladesh, Belgium, Brazil, Canada, Columbia, Czech/Slovak Republics, Denmark, Egypt, Finland, France, Ghana, India, Ireland, Jordan, Kenya, Luxembourg, Nepal, Netherlands, New Zealand, Nigeria, Norway, Poland, Portugal, Russia, Spain, Sweden, Switzerland, Tunisia, Ukraine, United Kingdom, United States, Venezuela

ITAC
(& UNAMIC)

Algeria, Argentina, Australia, Austria, Bangladesh, Belgium, Brunei, Bulgaria, Cameroon, Canada, Chile, Colombia, Egypt, Fiji, France, Germany, Ghana, Hungary, India, Indonesia, Ireland, Italy, Japan, Jordan, Kenya, Malaysia, Morocco, Nepal, New Zealand, Nigeria, Norway, Pakistan, Philippines, Poland, Russia, Senegal, Singapore, Sweden, Thailand, Tunisia, United Kingdom, United States, Uruguay

OSOM

Australia, Bangladesh, Belgium, Botswana, Canada, France, Germany, Greece, Egypt, Kuwait, Italy, India, Malaysia, Morocco, New Zealand, Nigeria, Norway, Pakistan, Romania, Saudi Arabia, South Korea, Sweden, Tunisia, Turkey, United Arab Emirates, United States, Zimbabwe

UMOZ

Argentina, Bangladesh, Botswana, Brazil, Canada, Cape Verde, Czech Republic, Egypt, Guinea-Bissau, Hungary, India, Italy, Malaysia, Portugal, Russia, Spain, Sweden, Zambia, Uruguay

UNITED NATIONS KOREAN COMMAND CONTINGENTS

UNOSOM FORCE STRUCTURE
(August 1993)

CONTINGENT	COMMITMENT
Australia	Two infantry battalions, naval forces, one fighter squadron
Belgium	One infantry battalion
Canada	One reinforced infantry brigade, naval forces, one squadron of transport aircraft
Denmark	Medical services
Ethiopia	One infantry battalion
France	One reinforced infantry battalion
Great Britain	Two infantry brigades, one armoured regiment, one combat engineer regiment, w/support troops, Far Eastern Fleet, two squadrons of aircraft
Greece	One infantry battalion, transport aircraft
Holland	One infantry battalion, naval forces
India	Medical services
Italy	Medical services
Luxembourg	One infantry company
New Zealand	One artillery regiment
Norway	Medical services
Philippines	One infantry battalion, one tank company
South Africa	One fighter squadron
Sweden	Medical services
Thailand	One infantry battalion, navel forces, air and naval transports
Turkey	One infantry brigade

Pakistan-23%	4,718	Nigeria	556
U.S. - 19%	3,881	Egypt	540
Italy - 12%	2,442	Turkey	316
Other contingents - 46%		Germany	288
Morocco	1,340	Romania	236
France	1,089	Botswana	203
Zimbabwe	987	Sweden	146
Belgium	966	Tunisia	143
Malaysia	873	Norway	138
United Arab Emirates	690	Kuwait	108
Saudi Arabia	678	Greece	101
Bangladesh	25		

NOTES:

1. UNOSOM HQ staff consists of an additional 390 Australian, Canadian, and New Zealand troops.

2. India and S. Korea have made troop commitments and sent advance parties.

3. A 1,158 man U.S. quick reaction force is on standby, but not under UN command.

4. This is an atypical UN force structure due to unique UNOSOM rules of engagement.

5. Total strength = 20,854 troops

UNITED NATIONS PEACE-KEEPING FORCE AND OBSERVER MISSIONS

FORCE/MISSION	DEPLOYMENT DATES	LOCATION	HEADQUARTERS	STRENGTH (MAX)
UN Truce Supervision Organization (UNTSO)	6/48-present	Israel	Jerusalem	572
UN Military Observer Group in India and Pakistan (UNMOGIP)	1/49-present	Jammu/ Kashmir	Rawalpindi/ Srinagar	102
First UN Emergency Force (UNEF I)	11/56-6/67	Sinai, Suez, Gaza	Gaza	6,073
UN Observer Group in Lebanon (UNOGIL)	6/58-12/58	Lebanon, Syria	Beirut	591
UN Operations in the Congo (ONUC)	7/60-6/64	Congo (Zaire)	Leopoldville (Kinshasa)	19,828
UN Security Force in West New Guinea (West Irian) (UNTEA/UNSF)	10/62-4/63	W. New Guinea	Hollandia (Jayaphra)	1,576
UN Yemen Observation Mission (UNYOM)	7/63-9/64	Yemen	San'a	189
UN Peace-keeping Force in Cyprus (UNFICYP)	3/64-present	Cyprus	Nicosia	6,411
Mission of the Representative of the Sec. Gen. in the Dominican Republic (DOMREP)	5/65-10/66	Dominican Republic	Santo Domingo	2
UN India-Pakistan Observation Mission (UNIPOM)	9/65-3/66	India/Pakistan	Lahore/Amritsa	96
Second UN Emergency Force (UNEF II)	10/73-7/79	Sinai, Suez	Ismailia	6,973
UN Disengagement Observer Force (UNDOF)	6/74-present	Golan Heights	Damascus, Syria	1,450
UN Interim Force in Lebanon (UNIFIL)	3/78-present	South Lebanon	Naqoura	7,000
UN Good Offices Mission in Afghanistan (UNGOMAP)	4/88-3/90	Afghanistan/ Pakistan	Kabul/ Islamabad	50
UN Iran-Iraq Military Observer Group (UNIIMOG)	8/88-2/91	Iraq/Iran	Baghdad/Teheran	399
UN Angola Verifcation Misson I (UNAVEM I)	1/89-6/91	Angola	Luanda	70
UN Transition Assistance Group (UNTAG)	4/89-3/90	Namibia	Windhoek	4,493
UN Observer Group in Central America (ONUCA)	11/89-1/92	Honduras	Tegucigalpa	1,098
UN Iraq-Kuwait Observation Mission (UNIKOM)	4/91-present	Iraq/Kuwait	Umm Qasr	686
UN Angola Verification Mission II (UNAVEM II)	6/91-present	Angola	Luanda	1,118
UN Observer Mission in El Salvador (ONUSAL)	7/91-present	El Salvador	San Salvador	1,146
UN Mission for the Referendum in Western Sahara (MINURSO)	9/64-present	W. Sahara	Laayoune	2,900
UN Advance Mission in Cambodia (UNAMIC)	10/91-3/92	Cambodia	Phnom Penh	N/A
UN Protection Force (UNPROFOR)	3/92-present	The Balkans	Zagreb, Croatia	23,000
UN Transitional Authority in Cambodia (UNTAC)	3/92-9/93	Cambodia	Phnom Penh	22,000
UN Operation in Somalia (UNOSOM)	4/92-present	Somalia	Mogadishu	20,854
UN Operation in Mozambique (ONUMOZ)	12/92-present	Mozambique	Maputo	7,500

GULF WAR ALLIES

ROUND TROOPS

¬ited States	35,000
¬audi Arabia	45,000
¬gypt	38,000
¬ited Kingdom	32,000
¬ria	21,000
¬ance	12,000
¬akistan	11,000
¬ulf Cooperation Council	10,000
¬angladesh	2,300
¬orocco	1,700
¬ger	500
¬enegal	500
¬zechoslovakia	200

OTHER ALLIES

Argentina	Greece
Australia	Italy
Belgium	Netherlands
Canada	New Zealand
Denmark	Norway
Germany	Spain

COUNTRIES PROVIDING ECONOMIC/HUMANITARIANN AID

Afghanistan	Malaysia
Austria	Philippines
Bulgaria	Portugal
Finland	Sierra Leone
Honduras	South Korea
Hungary	Sweden
Iceland	Taiwan
Japan	Turkey
Luxembourg	USSR

¬tes sur les planches en couleur

¬ L'Autriche participe à l'UNTSO depuis 1967. Remarquez l'épaulette bilingue ¬'ONU, le béret bleu et le badge métallique standards ainsi que le fusil Steyr ¬G. **A2** La Suède contribue de manière importante à l'UNTSO depuis 1948. ¬portent un calot bleu à la place du béret et un casque où les lettres 'UN' sont ¬tes ainsi qu'un badge de la carte mondiale de l'ONU. Les brassards ont un ¬gne suédois national et celui de l'ONU. L'arme est le M45 Carl Gustav. **A3** ¬ troupes polonaises participent à l'UNDOF, UNIMOG, UNTAG, ¬IKOM, MINURSO, UNPROFOR et UNTAC. Ce jeune officier au Moyen- ¬ent porte un uniforme polonais de camouflage et le calot bleu, mais le ¬tywka de camouflage était également très utilisé. Le brassard porte l'insigne ¬onal et le nom. **A4** Badge de béret des services médicaux UNTSO. **A5** Badge ¬ béret du contingent canadien UNEF.

¬ Les troupes britanniques fournissent la majorité des troupes d'UNFICYP à ¬ypre depuis les années 60. Cette récente recrue des troupes porte l'uniforme de ¬mouflage mis au point durant la Guerre du Golfe avec couvre-chef et insigne ¬que de l'ONU. **B2** Entre 1975 et 1979 le Shah d'Iran détacha des troupes à ¬NDOF. Ce soldat porte le rare uniforme de camouflage en deux tons de vert, ¬s insigne de l'ONU, et porte le fusil G3. **B3** La Finlande a énormément ¬tribué aux opérations de l'ONU depuis 1956. Ce soldat porte le calot bleu de ¬NU avec insigne bilingue et l'insigne national et celui de l'ONU sur un ¬ssard. Le fusil est le M62 finnois. **B4** Badge de béret d'officier en torsade ¬rgent. **B5** Badge d'officier d'aviation de l'ONU en torsade dorée sur fond ¬nc.

¬ Étant donné sa taille, l'armée de Fidji a pris une part énorme dans les ¬rations de l'ONU et a perdu beaucoup d'hommes. Ce soldat UNIFIL au ¬ban porte à l'épaule gauche l'insigne national et de rang. Son gilet pare-balles ¬vert en bleu est du type US PASGT. L'insigne de l'ONU est portée (non ¬ble ici) à l'épaule gauche. **C2** Le Ghana envoie un bataillon à l'ONU au Liban ¬uis 1979. Il porte un casque allemand, un gilet pare-balles de camouflage, un ¬talon de camouflage pour forêt et porte le fusil G3. **C3** Les norvégiens, de ¬nds participants à l'UNIFIL, portent leur treillis standard avec le béret et ¬signe de l'ONU et un gilet pare-balles US PASGT en camouflage forêt. **C4** ¬ge de béret du personnel de communications UNIFIL. **C5** Badge de béret du ¬ice en campagne de l'ONU.

¬ Sergent du génie, armée australienne, qui porte un uniforme de camouflage ¬ralien avec l'insigne national et de l'ONU sur un brassard. L'insigne de rang, ¬é ici, est porté sur l'épaule droite. **D2** Singapour a envoyé des troupes à ¬NTAG en Namibie, à l'UNIKOM au Kuwait et à l'UNTAC au Cambodge. ¬niforme de camouflage en forêt cambodgien est porté. Remarquez le gilet ¬e-balles recouvert en bleu et le béret avec son badge en tissu. **D3** Uniforme de ¬ouflage en forêt vénézuélien. calot bleu avec insigne bilingue, ¬blème national à l'épaule gauche et fusil FN FAL. **D4** Badge métallique de ¬t standard de l'ONU. **D5** Badge de béret d'officier en torsade or brodée sur ¬ laine blanche.

Farbtafeln

A1 Österreich leistet seit 1967 einen Beitrag zur UNTSO. Man beachte die zweisprachigen UN-Schulterembleme, das blaue Barett in der UN-Standardausführung mit Metallbzeichen und das Steyr AUG-Gewehr. **A2** Schweden spielt seit 1948 bei der UNTSO eine wichtige Rolle. Anstelle des Baretts tragen die Schweden die blaue Mütze sowie Helme, auf die 'UN' aufgemalt ist, und das UN-Abzeichen mit der Weltkarte. Die Armbinden tragen das schwedische Nationalemblem sowie das UN-Abzeichen. Bei der Waffe handelt es sich um die Carl Gustav M45. **A3** Polnische Truppen stellten ein Kontingent für die UNDOF, UNIMOG, UNTAG, UNIKOM, MINURSO, UNPROFOR und die UNTAC. Der hier abgebildete rangniedrige Offizier im Nahen Osten trägt die Tarnuniform, die während des Golfkrieges entstand, obgleich auch die Tarn-*Rogatywka* populär war. Auf der Armbinde befindet sich das Nationalemblem und der Name. **A4** Das Barettabzeichen der Sanitätstruppe der UNTSO. **A5** Das Barettabzeichen des kanadischen Truppenkontingents der UNEF.

B1 Britische Truppen machen seit den sechziger Jahren den Großteil der UNFICYP-Truppen in Zypern aus. Das hier abgebildete jüngere Truppenmitglied trägt die Tarnuniform, die während des Golfkrieges entstand, sowie Kopfbedeckung und Abzeichen in UN-Standardausführung. **B2** Zwischen 1975 und 1979 entsandte der Schah von Iran Truppen an die UNDOF; dieser Soldat trägt die seltene Tarnuniform in zwei Grüntönen, ohne UN-Abzeichen und trägt das G3-Gewehr. **B3** Finnland trägt seit 1956 erheblich zu UN-Einsätzen bei; dieser Soldat trägt die blaue UN-Mütze mit zweisprachigem Abzeichen sowie das UN-Abzeichen auf der Armbinde. Beim Gewehr handelt es sich um das finnische M62. **B4** Barettabzeichen eines Silberbullion-Offiziers. **B5** Gold auf weißes Abzeichen eines Fliegeroffiziers der UN.

C1 Verglichen mit ihrer Größe hat die Armee von Fidschi ein beträchtliches Engagement bei UNO-Einsätzen und mußte schwere Verluste hinnehmen. Dieser UNIFIL-Soldat im Libanon hat auf der rechten Schulter das Nationalemblem und die Rangabzeichen; seine blau überzogene Panzerweste entspricht dem amerikanischen PASGT-Muster; das UN-Abzeichen wird auf der linken Schulter getragen (hier nicht sichtbar). **C2** Ghana entsendet seit 1979 eine Bataillonsgruppe zur UN im Libanon. Auf der Abbildung sieht man einen deutschen Helm, DPM-Tarnpanzerweste, Hosen im Waldtarnmuster und das G3-Gewehr. **C3** Die Norweger leisten einen erheblichen Beitrag zur UNIFIL und tragen ihre Standardarbeitsuniform mit dem Barett und dem Abzeichen der UN sowie amerikanische Panzerwesten des Type PASGT in Waldtarnmuster. **C4** Barettabzeichen der Fernmeldemannschaft der UNIFIL. **C5** Barettabzeichen der UN-Feldtruppen.

D1 Feldwebel der Pioniere der australischen Armee in australischer Tarnuniform mit UN-Abzeichen und Nationalemblem auf der Armbinde; die hier nicht sichtbaren Rangabzeichen werden auf der rechten Schulter getragen. **D2** Singapur entsandte Truppen an die UNTAG in Namibia, an die UNIKOM in

E Le centre d'entraînement nordique en Finlande entraîne les troupes destinées aux opérations de l'ONU provenant des quatre nations nordiques et de la Suisse. E1 Emblème NTC. E2 Infirmier suédois, à gauche, s'entraîne à traiter un soldat finnois (premier plan) sous la supervision d'un officier suisse. Le Suédois porte un uniforme de camouflage M1990 et une combinaison suisse de camouflage une pièce M73. E3 Police militaire finnoise à l'entraînement avec un chien de garde. E4 Emblème national finnois.

F1 Soldat du bataillon ukrainien à Sarajevo qui porte un uniforme de camouflage de type soviétique avec l'insigne national à l'épaule de l'ONU. Casque bleu, gilet pare-balles vert et fusil AK-74S tous d'origine soviétique. F2 Uniforme espagnol de camouflage en forêt, béret ONU avec badge en tissu, insigne national sur les deux épaules, fusil CETME L. F3 Ce soldat d'infanterie du contingent le plus important dans l'ancienne Yougoslavie porte un casque britannique et un gilet pare-balles recouverts en bleu, un uniforme DPM et un insigne britannique et ONU à l'épaule. F4 Treillis standard français 'satin 300' avec insigne national sur l'épaule droite, casque bleu M1978 F1 et gilet pare-balles recouvert de camouflage: l'un des trois types utilisés. F5 La toute première contribution des Etats-Unis aux forces terrestres des 'bérets bleus' en Macédoine. Ce soldat de la Brigade de Berlin porte un casque PASGT peint en bleu avec un uniforme BDU blanc pour forêts de l'ONU et matériel ALICE. Il porte un M249 SAW.

G1 Chemise néerlandaise de camouflage à trois poches, emblème national et insigne bilingue de l'ONU à l'épaule gauche. G2 Bulgarien au Cambodge avec un uniforme de camouflage bulgarien à éclaboussures sans insigne de l'ONU. G3 Major du génie JSDF qui porte un uniforme de camouflage 'flektar' avec un emblème national en couleur à l'épaule gauche et l'insigne national ONU à l'épaule droite, ruban 'Japon' à droite sur la poitrine et calot bleu à visière avec insigne ONU. G4 Uniforme américain léger de camouflage en forêt avec la combinaison habituelle d'insignes national et ONU et casque bleu. G5 Uniforme de camouflage copié sur place ressemblant au type 'ERDL' américain avec tous les insignes brodés sur le tissu assorti et aucun emblème ONU.

H1 Parachutiste italien portant le camouflage pour désert mis au point pour la guerre du Golfe (bien que l'Italie n'ait pas fourni de troupes pour ce conflit) et matériel Ephod israélien. Il porte le fusil BM-59. H2 Casque britannique avec housse fabriquée en Corée, uniforme de camouflage coréen avec emblème national et insigne de rang Arif et gilet pare-balles Point Blank. H3 Béret et écharpe ONU, uniforme pakistanais marron sans insigne en couleur. Par la suite on leur fournit des casques bleus américains M1 et un uniforme de camouflage pour forêts avec un gilet pare-balles de camouflage forêt. H4 NCO du 1er bataillon de parachutistes belges qui porte un béret avec un badge d'unité, un T-shirt réglementaire, un gilet pare-balles britannique avec housse désert et un pantalon de camouflage belge 1958. Il porte un fusil FNC. H5 Premier déploiement allemand à l'étranger depuis 1945 représenté par un NCO de haut grade qui porte un béret ONU avec un badge en tissu, un uniforme de camouflage 'flektar', un brassard à l'épaule gauche pour l'emblème national et le nom et un insigne ONU bilingue.

I1 Pilote sud-africain de Mustang qui porte un casque de pilote avec un costume de pilotage d'été 1944 AN-S-31A, un gilet de sauvetage B-5, des chaussures de service en croûte et un masque à oxygène A-14. I2 Marines qui portent un treillis 1944 HBT et des housses de casque de camouflage tachetées. I3 Insigne d'épaule de l'équipe de combat UN Airborne, US 187ème régiment. I4 Insigne d'épaule du QG du commandement de l'ONU. I5 Insigne d'épaule de la Zone de Sécurité Commune. I6 Ecusson de l'ONU.

J1 Soldat des forces spéciales syriennes qui porte un uniforme soviétique L-1 NBC et un masque SHMS avec fusil AKM. J2 Uniforme français de camouflage de désert à quatre poches avec décorations de parade de l'Infanterie Marine. J3 Casque américain M1 avec housse réversible, uniforme de camouflage désert à six couleurs fabriqué en Corée, matériel américain ALICE, bottes de désert, masque à gaz et fusil G3. J4 Uniforme de camouflage à trois couleurs remarqué dans de nombreuses armées du Golfe avec béret noir et insigne de rang sur les boucles d'épaule.

K Badges de poche des Nations-Unies. Il s'agit de quelques exemples des nombreuses variétés fabriquées sur place ou dans le pays d'origine. Voir les légendes en anglais.

L Médailles de service aux Nations-Unies et (L7a–s) rubans pour les différentes opérations portés avec la Médaille Standard (L5 et L6). Voir les légendes en anglais.

Kuwait und an die UNTAC in Kambodscha. Hier ist die Waldtarnuniform a Singapur abgebildet; man beachte die blau bezogene Panzerweste und das Ba mit Stoffabzeichen. D3 Waldtarnuniform aus Venezuela, blaue UN-Mütze zweisprachigem Abzeichen, Nationalemblem auf der linken Schulter und F FAL-Gewehr. D4 Von der UN allgemein ausgegebenes Barettabzeichen Metall. D5 Barettabzeichen eines Goldbullion-Offiziers, auf weißen Wolls aufgestickt.

E Das nordische Trainingszentrum in Finnland bildet für die UN bestimm Truppen aus allen vier nordischen Ländern und aus der Schweiz aus. E1 NT Emblem. E2 Schwedische Ordonnanz, links, übt die medizinische Versorgung einem finnischen Soldaten (im Vordergrund) und wird von einem Schwei Offizier beaufsichtigt. Der Schwede trägt die Tarnuniform M1990, der Schwei den einteiligen Tarnoverall M73. E3 Finnische Militärpolizei beim Training einem Wachhund. E4 Finnisches Nationalemblem.

F1 Ukrainischer Bataillonssoldat in Sarajewo in einer Tarnuniform sowjetisch Stils mit UN-Abzeichen und Nationalemblem; der blau gestrichene Helm, grüne Panzerweste und das AK-74S-Gewehr sind alle sowjetischer Herkunft. Spanische Waldtarnuniform, UN-Barett mit Stoffabzeichen, Nationalemble auf beiden Schultern, CETME L-Gewehr. F3 Dieser Infanterist aus d größten Truppenkontingent im ehemaligen Jugoslawien trägt einen b überzogenen britischen Helm und eine Panzerweste, DPM-Uniform und Schulterabzeichen der UN und Großbritanniens. F4 Französi Arbeitsuniform der Standardausführung 'Satin 300' mit Nationalemblem auf rechten Schulter, blauer Helm M1978 F1 und mit Tarnfarben bezoge Panzerweste – einer der drei verwendeten Typen. F5 Der allererste B g der Vereinigten Staaten zu den 'Blaubarett'-Bodentruppen der UN folgte in Makedonien. Dieser Soldat der Berlin Brigade trägt einen au angestrichenen PASGT-Helm mit der Aufschrift 'UN' in weiß, BDU-W uniform und ALICE-Ausrüstung; er hat ein M249 SAW. G1 Holla sches Tarnhemd mit drei Taschen, Nationalemblem und zweisprachiges UN-Ab en auf der linken Schulter. G2 Bulgare in Kambodscha in der sowjeti schen Tarnuniform im Splittermuster ohne UN-Abzeichen. G3 JSDF-Pionieri Tarnanzug 'Flektar' mit mehrfarbigem Nationalemblem auf der linken S lter, zweisprachiges UN-Abzeichen auf der rechten Schulter. Er trägt das an'-Band auf der rechten Brust und eine blaue Schirmmütze mit -Abzeichen. G4 Amerikanische leichte W ldtarnuniform mit der üblichen Kombination des Nationalemble und des UN-Abzeichens und blaue Mütze. G5 Vor Ort kopierte Tarn orm, die dem amerikanischen 'ERDL'-Modell ähnelt. Alle Abzeichen s auf passenden Stoff aufgestickt und sie hat keine UN-Abzeichen. H1 D r italienische Fallschirmjäger trägt den Wüstentarnanzug, der im Anschlu den Golfkrieg entwickelt wurde (obgleich Italien keine Truppen ins Krisenge entsandte), und israelische Ephod-Ausrüstung; er hat ein BM-59-Gewe ei sich. H2 Britischer Helm in Korea hergestelltem Bezug, UN-Barett mi rm aus koreanischer Produktion mit Nationalemblem und dem Rangabzeich rif sowie Panzerweste Point Blank. H3 UN-Barett und Schal, hellbraune Pa ni-Uniform mit farbigen Abz ichen. Später wurden blau gestrichene US-Helme M1 und Wald-beziehungs e Wüstentarnbekleidung mit Panzerwesten im Waldtarnmuster ausgegeben. H4 Ü fizier des 1. belgischen Fallschirmjägerbataillons im Barett und Abzeichen r Einheit. Er trägt ein ausgegebenes T-Shirt, eine britische Panze te mit Wüstenbezug und belgische Tarnhosen des Modells 1958. Er trägt ein FNC-Gewehr bei sich. H5 Deutschlands erste Truppenstationierung im sland seit 1945, dargestellt an diesem Oberfeldwebel im UN-Barett mit offabzeichen, 'Flektar'-Tarnuniform, Armbinde an der linken Schulter mit d Nationalemblem, dem Namen und dem zweisprachigen UN-Abzeichen.

I1 Dieser südafrikanische Mustang-Pilot trägt einen harten Fliegerhelm einen 1944er AN-S-31A Sommerfliegeranzug, eine 1944er B-5 Schwimmwe Dienstschuhe 'mit der rauhen Seite nach außen' und eine A-14 Sauerstoffma I2 Marineinfanteristen in der 1944er HBT-Arbeitsuniform und den beids tragbaren, getupften Helmtarnbezügen. I3 Schulterabzeichen der Kampftru des 187. US-Regiments, UN Airborne. I4 Schulterabzeichen der U Kommandostelle. I5 Schulterabzeichen der Gemeinsamen Sicherheitszone. UN–Abzeichen.

J1 Soldat der syrischen Sondertruppen trägt einen sowjetischen L-1 Anzug und die ShMS-Maske sowie ein AKM-Gewehr. J2 Französis Wüstentarnuniform mit vier Taschen mit Paradeschmuck der Marineinfa J3 Amerikanischer M1-Helm mit beidseitig tragbarem Bezug; sechsfart Wüstentarnuniform koreanischer Machart; amerikanische ALICE-Ausrüst Wüstenstiefel, Gasmaske und G3-Gewehr. J4 Dreifarbige Tarnuniform, die vielen Truppen im Golf getragen wurde, schwarzes Barett und Rangabzeic auf den Schulterklappen.

K Abzeichen auf den Taschen der Uniform der Vereinten Nationen. Hier s einige der vielen unterschiedlichen Ausführungen abgebildet, die auf nation oder regionaler Ebene produziert werden. Siehe englischsprachige Erläuterun zu den Farbtafeln.

L Dienstmedaille der Vereinten Nationen und (L7a–s) Ordensbänder verschiedene Einsätze, die mit der Standardmedaille (L5 & L6) getragen were Siehe englischsprachige Erläuterungen zu den Farbtafeln.